WORLD ON A STRING

HELANE ZEIGER

THE HOW-TO YO-YO BOOK

PHOTOGRAPHY BY HOWARD BRAINEN

Library of Congress Cataloging in Publication Data
Zeiger, Helane.
       World on a String.

       Bibliography: p
       Includes index.
       1. Yo-yos. I. Title.
GV1216.Z45   1979   796.2   78-24486
ISBN: 0-9622941-0-1

Second Printing 1989.
Published by TK Yo-Yos Ltd., 2383 California Street, San Francisco, CA 94115.

Manufactured in the United States of America
Library of Congress Catalog Card Number: 78-24486
International Standard Book Number: 0-9622941-0-1 (paper)

Front cover photograph by Alan Krosnick, San Francisco.

Design by Howard Solotroff

Photographs copyrighted by Howard Brainen, except where noted.

Mr. YO-YO Duncan diagrams from The Art of Yo-Yo Playing, copyright 1950,
Donald F. Duncan. Used by permission of Flambeau Products Corporation.

Contents

Acknowledgments

Fondly, I thank my agent, Marcia Amsterdam, and my husband, Ron Zeiger, for their continual encouragement, endless patience, and good advice during the ups and downs of writing a how-to yo-yo book.

Without the additional support and knowledge of the "yo-yo community", this book might never have come to be. I especially thank Dan Volk and Bill deBoisblanc for contributing their extraordinary skill as demonstrated on some of the pages of this book and for making their prize yo-yo memorabilia available to me. I am also indebted to Tom Kuhn, Beth Frazier, and Michelle Lewis for sharing their yo-yo treasures, and to Gus Somera and the "Duncan" Yo-Yo Pros for teaching and inspiring us all.

I am particularly grateful to Donald F. Duncan, Jr., and Dale Oliver for the photographs they provided and the pleasant two hours we spent talking about the history of yo-yos, and to William H.

Schlee, Jr., and Doug Bahringer for also furnishing photographs and information about yo-yos.

I would also like to express my appreciation to Howard Brainen, who through the lens of his camera, captured more than spinning yo-yos, and to George Post for the many hours he spent printing these fine photographs.

These acknowledgments would not be complete without thanking Judith Goldhaber who introduced me to Marcia Amsterdam who suggested I write a how-to yo-yo book. And I did. Thank you, all.

Foreword from a Yo-Yo Pro

Just before graduating from P.S. 86 in the Bronx, my cousin Lois wrote this verse in my autograph album:

Not a worry, not a care,
With the yo-yo you've quite a flare,
It's "Heleena Goldeena" doing the
    Shooting Star,
Best Wishes, Good Luck, may you
    rocket far!

Neither my cousin nor I would have believed then that I would be rocketing far with my yo-yo 25 years later as one of 4 women yo-yo professionals in the United States and demonstrating my "flare" with the yo-yo to thousands of children as the "Duncan Yo-Yo Lady"!

How did I acquire this unique talent? Back in the 1950's when other girls my age were rocking dolls in carriages and practicing for future motherhood, I was rocking my "baby" in its yo-yo cradle, following the "Duncan Yo-Yo Man" from the city street corner to city street corner, and watching him go through his yo-yo repertory until I had mastered all the beginning tricks and many of the more difficult ones. After winning several first place badges in yo-yo contests in front of my local candy store, the "Yo-Yo Man" awarded me a "Junior Instructor" patch, which entitled me to teach *Walking-the-Dog, Skin-the-Cat, The Creeper,* and other basic tricks to kids in my neighborhood.

First place badges came in various shapes and sizes.

Berkeley, California, youngsters show a fascination for the yo-yo.

While other kids dutifully practiced scales on the piano or did their homework every evening, out in the hall of my apartment building I would work up some new trick I wanted to teach them. I would whirl my yo-yo *Around-the-World* or *Skyrocket* it up to the ceiling by the end of the yo-yo-string, catching it again in my pocket, all the time dreaming of becoming a "Duncan Yo-Yo Professional" when I grew up.

Now that I've realized my childhood ambition and have become a "Yo-Yo Pro," I teach many, many children and adults how to do tricks with their yo-yos. But there are millions of other yo-yo enthusiasts whom I will never help learn how to yo-yo face-to-face.

I have written *World on a String: The How-To Yo-Yo Book* with the hope that it will bring hours of enjoyment to all those who love to play with yo-yos as much as I do and that this book will be an entertaining and informative guide for people of all ages that I cannot instruct in person. *Happy yo-yoing!*

Helane Zeiger
"Yo-Yo Professional"

1

The History of Yo-Yos
500 B.C. to 1979 A.D.

"The common yo-yo," Frank Conroy recalls in *Stop Time,* a memoir of his boyhood and adolescence, "is crudely made, with a thick shank between two widely spaced wooden disks. The string is knotted . . . to the shank. With such an instrument nothing can be done except simple up-down movement."

Originating in China in most ancient times, the first yo-yos were probably very much like Conroy's description. In ancient Greece, where they were more than likely a children's toy as well, they were made of wood, metal, and terra cotta. Upon reaching adolescence, young Greeks would offer up ceramic discs, exact replicas of their real childhood toy, to their favorite gods. These votive substitutes, as well as a piece of decorated pottery dating from the classical period in Greece showing a youngster in a headband and tunic playing with a yo-yo, are on display in the Museum of Athens.

A hand-painted picture of a girl in a red dress doing tricks with her yo-yo appears on a miniature box from Kashmir, India,

Ancient Greek terracotta yo-yo (left). (Courtesy of the Metropolitan Museum of Art, Fletcher Fund, 1928.)

Decorated terracotta disks painted on white ground from ancient Greece (left and right below). (Courtesy of the Metropolitan Museum of Art, Fletcher Fund, 1928.)

WORLD ON A STRING

Vase painting dated about 500 B.C. shows a young citizen of Greece playing with a yo-yo.

dated 1765.

Drawings of objects in the shapes of yo-yos have even been seen in ancient Egyptian temples.

In 1790 the yo-yo made its way from the Orient to Europe, where it became popular among the British and French aristocracy and inherited some new names. In England the yo-yo was sometimes known as the bandalore, quiz, or Prince of Wales's toy. A painting from the late 1700s, which hangs in the British Museum, shows King George IV, then Prince of Wales, whirling a bandalore.

In France, the yo-yo picked up the nicknames *incroyable* and *l'émigrette*. It was said that the Dauphin, a son of Marie Antoinette and Louis XVI, was very skillful with *l'emigrette*. A picture of the young prince in the Municipal Museum at Auxerre shows him playing with a yo-yo. During the French Revolution, yo-yos made of ivory and other precious materials were a pastime of the upperclass nobles. The Reign of Terror forced these nobles, known as *émigrés,* to flee Paris. Thus , the French version of the yo-yo, *l'émigrette,* was named after them.

The credit for naming and perfecting the yo-yo, however, belongs to the people of the Philippines. In the sixteenth century jungle fighters from that land attached thick ropes, twenty feet in length, to primitively made yo-yos and used these unique weapons to stun their prey or enemy. As the yo-yo evolved into a toy, natives of the Philippines became expert at making and using them. Fathers would

André Boniface Louis Mirabeau, French émigré, plays with a yo-yo.

WORLD ON A STRING

traditionally carve yo-yos for their sons out of mahogany or the horn of water buffalo. The game soon became a national pastime in the Philippines.

Since most Filipinos play with yo-yos from childhood, it is not surprising that the toy first was introduced into the United States by a Filipino, Pedro Flores. It immediately was called "yo-yo" in this country , the Tagalog, or Filipino, word meaning "come-come" or "to return."

Gus Somera, a Filipino who has demonstrated "Duncan" yo-yos for almost fifty years, recalled the all-Filipino crew that helped Flores popularize yo-yos like the original one Flores whittled in a Santa Barbara hotel room in the 1920s. "Pedro Flores had the first yo-yo company in Los Angeles. With him was Alfred Mendoza, George Somera, Chris Somera, Ernesto Valdez, Fortunato Anunciacion, and Bob Rola."

Donald F. Duncan, the man who is credited with starting the yo-yo fad in the

The famous "Our Gang" kids helped Donald F. Duncan promote his product in the early thirties. (Courtesy of Donald F. Duncan, Jr.)

An orangutan from the Chicago Zoo also popularized "Duncan" yo-yo in the early thirties. (Courtesy of Donald F. Duncan, Jr.)

United States, saw his first yo-yo while on a business trip to San Francisco in 1927 or 1928. "It looked like a potato on a string," he recalled. "It didn't do anything; it just went up and down."

What Duncan also saw was that the yo-yo could be a very marketable toy if it could do more than that. Proving himself to be a merchandising genius, so much so that today's word "Duncan" still is synonymous with "yo-yo," he introduced the slip-string, which looped around the axle of the yo-yo instead of being knotted to it. This enables the yo-yo to "stick" at the bottom of the string and return only when the string is give a slight jerk. While the yo-yo "sticks" or "sleeps," intricate tricks can be executed.

WORLD ON A STRING

City champions, many proudly wearing the highly-prized sweater-vest, gather in San Diego, California, for the 1954 state finals. (Photo courtesy of the deBoisblanc family.)

Sweaters, patches, plaques, and trophies were some of the prizes awared to local winners in the 1950s.

Next, Duncan bought the idea of the yo-yo from Flores, and patented the modern toy (Patent Number 300504) under the name "Yo-Yo." He established the Duncan Yo-Yo Company and created the "Duncan Yo-Yo Professionals." Many of Flores' men went to work for Duncan.

Throughout the United States they taught and demonstrated yo-yo tricks to promote sales.

As young people across the nation caught onto the tricks, the "Pros" held local competitions and city and state championships to discover the best yo-yo players.

As the "Pros" continued to teach tricks and run contests, competitions and prizes grew in size. At first a sweater-vest with a large blue and red patch embroidered with the words "Duncan Yo-Yo Winner" was a coveted prize. But by the end of the 1940s it was not unusual for a state or regional champion to receive a large sum of money, a trip to Hawaii, or a bicycle.

Beth Moorehead Frazier took second place in 1959 and 1961 in the California State Finals and won a total of $500. She recalled, "It was fantastic to win the money. I used it to help pay for my orthodontic work."

Bill deBoisblanc, runner-up in the 1955 California State Finals, won $250 for second place. "I was a little disappointed," he remembered. "That was the first year the girls' championship was run simultaneously. The year before the second place price was $500. But the next year, half of it went to the girl runner-up. And

Bill deBoisblanc does a perfect Rock-the-Baby to take first place in the 1952 city championship in Inglewood, California. (Photo courtesy of the deBoisblanc family.)

Beth Moorehead accepts her prize money from Bob Allen (center), along with other winners in the 1959 California State Championship held in Sacramento. (Courtesy of Beth Moorehead Frazier.)

Bill happily receives an enormous "Duncan" patch and the opportunity to compete in the 1952 state finals. A not-so-content runner-up is awarded a giant "Duncan" yo-yo. (Photo courtesy of the deBoisblanc family.)

I didn't even spend the money. I banked it for college."

Many of the local contests and state championships throughout the thirties, forties, and fifties were run by the most well-known "Duncan Yo-Yo Professional,"

Gus Somera. Born in 1912 in the Philippines, Gus came to Chicago in 1929 to attend high school and to work for the Duncan Yo-Yo Company. Today, 49 years later, he is still on the road demonstrating "Duncan" yo-yos.

Over the years, Gus has entertained millions of kids with their favorite tricks, *Rock-the-Baby, Walking-the-Dog,* and *Loop-the-Loop.* "Kids don't like the complicated tricks," Gus says, "because they can't do them." But Gus can do them, and his favorite trick is to keep the yo-yo spinning as he goes from *Rock-the-Baby* into *Ferris Wheel,* then *Brain Twister,* and ends up with *Reach-for-the-Moon.* He also delights in giving some of the old tricks new names. *Skyrocket,* for example, has been renamed *Sputnik.*

Gus prefers to do the tricks with the new plastic "Duncan" yo-yos rather than the old wooden ones. He recommends that kids begin with the "Duncan" Butterfly or Imperial. "With these yo-yos it is easier for kids to learn," he says. Adults who played with yo-yos will remember Gus as the man who carved their initials along with a palm tree into their wooden yo-yos. "We had to learn to carve to help the sale," Gus states. "But the wooden yo-yos

Gus Somera performs Crazy Cradle with the yo-yo he likes best. (Tom Young, photographer.)

broke too easily and were too light. Today's plastic yo-yos are better because they're heavier."

When the Duncan Yo-Yo Company went bankrupt in 1965 because the demand for yo-yos was greater than the supply, Gus Somera used his flexible wrists to flip eggs in a restaurant on State Street in Chicago. But he was back flipping yo-yos five years later when a plastics company, Flambeau, located in Baraboo, Wisconsin, bought the "Duncan" name and launched the yo-yo revival.

Under the trademark "Duncan," the Flambeau Plastics company manufactures 11 different models of yo-yos, including the Butterfly, with its rounded halves inside and its flat surfaces outside, and the Professional, which is a lighter, more streamlined yo-yo.

Doug Bahringer, Promotion Coordinator for "Duncan" Toy Division of the Flambeau Plastics Company,

"Duncan Pros" (from left to right) James DuRuz, Tom McCoy, Donna Walsh, Helane Zeiger, Gus Somera, Mike Steele, and George Humphreys take a break from their pre-promotion meeting to do some yo-yo tricks. (Tom Young, Photographer.)

supervises the "Duncan Yo-Yo Professionals." On the road 10 months of the year along with Gus Somera are: Tom McCoy, who taught himself how to yo-yo while in college and says, "The hardest trick is the one you're working on"; George Humphreys, who is 19 years old, the youngest demonstrator, and calls himself "The Yo-Yo Kid"; Mike Steele, who caught the yo-yo fever from Carl Bates, a former "Pro," and uses yo-yos in his magic act as well; Lance Lynch, who loves to make kids smile with his yo-yo; and James "Dev" DuRuz, who picked up yo-yoing from Bill Oliver, another past "Duncan Pro."

Dev's favorite is the *Roller Coaster,* which starts with *Double or Nothing,* goes into *Brain Twister,* then *Man on the Flying Trapeze,* and ends with a reverse *Forward Pass.*

Only four women in the United States have demonstrated yo-yos professionally. Linda Sengpiel runs Super-Sonic Yo-Yo Promotions in Cuyahoga Falls, Ohio and entertains at parties, picnics, and conventions. In Mexico in 1973, Loxy Oliver was the first woman to demonstrate yo-yos for Flambeau Plastics. With her husband, Dale Oliver, Loxy now works for Duracraft, Inc., manufacturer of the PRO-YO. A "Duncan Yo-Yo Professional" in 1977 and 1978, Donna Walsh learned to yo-yo from James DuRuz and likes yo-yoing in the schools where the children are a captive audience. Helane Zeiger, who won local yo-yo contests in the Bronx in the fifties and had her yo-yo carved by Gus Somera in front of her old neighborhood candy store in 1977, got her job as a "Duncan" Pro by answering an ad in the San Francisco Chronicle which read "Yo-Yo demonstrator wanted. Must be adept at handling a yo-yo."

Although "Duncan" yo-yos are the most well-known, Flambeau is not the only company making yo-yos. Wilfred H. Schlee, Jr., former vice president of the Duncan Yo-Yo Company, now is in charge

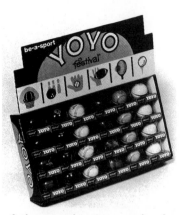

The "Be-A-Sport" line of yo-yos (left). (Courtesy of Union Wadding company, "Festival" yo-yos.)

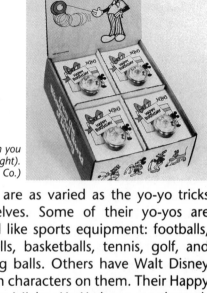

These "Festival" yo-yos wish you "Happy Birthday" (right). (Courtesy of Union Wadding Co.)

of the production and sales of "Festival" yo-yos, a division of Union Wadding Company in Pawtucket, Rhode Island. Before becoming a part of Union Wadding, Schlee manufactured yo-yos for Cheerio Toys and Games, Inc. Duncan bought out the Cheerio line in 1960, and Schlee became a vice president of the company. He left Duncan in 1964 to form Festival Products, Inc., which Union Wadding acquired two years later.

The shapes and designs of "Festival" yo-yos are as varied as the yo-yo tricks themselves. Some of their yo-yos are shaped like sports equipment: footballs, baseballs, basketballs, tennis, golf, and bowling balls. Others have Walt Disney cartoon characters on them. Their Happy Birthday Mickey Yo-Yo has a see-through "happy birthday" theme, and the Game Yo-Yo is a professional model with a see-through baseball, pinball, golf, or tic-tac-toe game. Also available is a book entitled Yo-Yo Secrets. Bob Rule, author of that yo-yo instruction book, is a past "Duncan Pro," who calls himself "Mister Yo-Yo."

After a 10-year absence from the yo-yo business, Donald F. Duncan, Jr., the son of the man who started the whole yo-yo craze, is once again manufacturing yo-yos. In 1965, when sales were at their peak, no one would have suspected that the Duncan Yo-Yo Company would go out of business. "But the demand for yo-yos was so great," Duncan Jr. remembers, "we just couldn't fill the orders and hadn't the capital to build another plant. The court had to sell the "Duncan" name, inventory, and yo-yo molds to the highest bidder, Flambeau Plastics, the former supplier of plastic for the Duncan Yo-Yo Company." At that time, Duncan Jr. moved to Arizona, where he became a manufacturer's representative for a saxophone company in Nogales and later a business representative for the Papago Indian tribe in Sells, Arizona.

The catchy word, "yo-yo," the Duncan family trademark, was in part responsible for the demise of the Duncan Yo-Yo Company. "Two competitors, Royal and Dell Plastics, tried to take the name away from us. These companies knew that using the word 'yo-yo' would increase their sales. This led to on and off court litigation to protect our trademark," Duncan Jr. recalls. "We also held on to

Following in his father's footsteps, Donald F. Duncan, manufacturers Pro-Yos. (Courtesy of Duracraft, Inc.)

Pro-Yo "the ultimate yo-yo," is designed for longer spin (above). (Courtesy of Duracraft, Inc.) Dale and Loxy Oliver perform Texas Star with "Pro-Yos" (right).

wood too long. Wood was becoming scarce and very expensive. We should have changed to making our yo-yos out of plastic earlier."

Now that the word "yo-yo" is the term commonly used by anyone referring to spinning return top, Donald F. Duncan, Jr., coined and registered another clever word, "Pro-Yo," for his late entry in the yo-yo field. But his yo-yo, manufactured at Duracraft, Inc., in Tucson, Arizona, might be the eventual winner of the race.

Dale Oliver, sales manager for Duracraft and former "Duncan Professional," maintains that the "Pro-Yo" sleeps, or spins, up to 50 percent longer than any existing yo-yo. That is due to the quality construction of the toy. Eighty percent of the weight of the "Pro-Yo" is in the rim so it acts like a fly wheel. A beveled hex-axle self-centers the string, allowing it to fall into a groove. The "Pro-Yo" has a brass axle, and the more expensive model, the Ultimate Pro-Yo, has a wooden axle. Both yo-yos have a customizing feature, a side lens that pops out and enables you to pop in your own design, picture, or emblem of your favorite team or school. The string is double-looped for play by beginners and can be changed easily to a single loop for more advanced yo-yo players.

Oliver states that there have been three major innovations in the modern history of the yo-yo:

"In 1958 when Wayne Lundberg, a past 'Duncan Professional,' helped create the Butterfly and Donald F. Duncan, Jr., named it; in 1960 when yo-yos began to be made of plastic; and in 1978 when Duracraft, Inc., introduced the 'Pro-Yo,' with its major weight distribution around the rim."

Dale Oliver, who has been a yo-yo professional for 25 years, holds 2 world records. In 1976 at the Annual Father's Day All-Wooden Yo-Yo Contest held in Seattle, Washington, Oliver, using a yo-yo that he designed himself, slept his custom yo-yo for 45 seconds for one record and sent it *Around-the-World* 27 times for another.

In the early fifties Jack Russell, who demonstrated "Duncan' yo-yos for a time after World War II, started the Russell Yo-Yo Company. Like Duncan, Russell relied on professional demonstrators to promote his Super and Professional models in countries outside the United States. Today, all but one of his professionals are foreign born. Demonstrating yo-yos all over the world for the Russell Yo-Yo Company are: José Jeraldo and brothers Alfonzo and Ivan Trujillo from Columbia, South America; Anna Chow from Hong Kong; Adsuko Tarahara from Tokyo, Japan (Chow and Tarahara are believed to be the best women pros in the world); Carmello Lopez from Spain; Javier Barroeta from Mexico; Manuel Valdez from the Philippines; Ben Tan from Singapore; and Davy Jones from Australia.

The only American in the Russell crew

is Dan Volk from San Francisco. Dan first got interested in yo-yos when a friend he met at summer camp taught him a few tricks. Afterward, he went to see the Duncan Champions, Fortunato Anunciacion, Barney Akers, George Somera, and Charlie Cerrano, when they came to his neighborhood in Cleveland, Ohio.

Dan's first yo-yo was a "Duncan" Tournament—"a wooden one, light blue with a white stripe across it," he recalls. "My friend Chuck Morris gave it to me and I still have it." With his light blue, striped "Duncan" Tournament yo-yo, Dan went on to win his neighborhood contest for the East Side of Cleveland and, finally, in 1960 the Cleveland City Championship.

As prizes Dan "got yo-yos, strings, patches, a plaque, a fishing set, and a portable black and white TV." In 1974 Dan became a professional because he "was getting too good to remain an amateur." Since then he has demonstrated

Dan Volk proudly displays one of his prizes and the yo-yo that brought him victory in Cleveland, Ohio.

yo-yos in Tokyo, Barcelona, and atop the Eiffel Tower in Paris.

Dan's most memorable experience as a yo-yo professional was as the performer in the film *33 Yo-Yo Tricks* by P. White, which was released in 1976 and won a prize in the Ann Arbor Film Festival. Prints of the film are available through New York, Boston and Cleveland libraries. Dan thoroughly enjoyed being in the movie and doing each one of the 33 tricks with amazing precision. He firmly believes that "the yo-yo is the greatest toy that ever was and ever will be!"

With funds from the National Endowment for the Arts and the Flambeau Plastics Company, John Bishop, an independent filmmaker from Boston, has just completed filming another movie with a yo-yo professional as the subject. His film is entitled *Yo-Yo Man* and shows a 76-year-old Nemo Concepcion, another former "Duncan Yo-Yo Professional," in action.

Lesser known names than "Festival," Russell, and Duncan, Jr., are trying to come up with a better yo-yo than the ones available today. Robert Blair of Watsonville, California, has invented a flying yo-yo

Tom Kuhn carefully weighs one of his hand-turned yo-yos.

with a propeller attached to it. He hopes to market his airplane wonder and call it the "Proper Yo-Yo." In his workshop at home, Tom Kuhn, a San Francisco dentist, produces handsome wooden yo-yos, some with interchangeable parts and all with fantastic spin. He calls his top-of-the-line model the No-Jive.

When the Duncan Yo-Yo Company went out of business in the sixties, Larry Sayer, a former world yo-yo champion and "Duncan" demonstrator, went into the yo-yo business for himself. He runs Sayco, a one-man company, out of a tiny building in Pawtucket, Rhode Island, selling about 100,000 yo-yos a year. He built several of the machines he uses, runs them, produces the finished product, and makes the sales. The finished product is a tournament yo-yo with a wooden axle. "Nothing plays as good as wood because of the co-efficient of friction," he says.

There's good reason for the great comeback of the yo-yo! People through the ages have been fascinated with the yo-yo and have enjoyed playing with it because it's a fun toy that always wants to return!

2

How Yo-Yos Are Made

Although 90 percent of all yo-yos manufactured today are made from plastics, for centuries yo-yos were made out of other materials. In the Philippines before the yo-yo was ever used as a toy, it was fashioned from rock and used as a weapon. Using a stone with a sharp point at the end, a slight groove was chiseled out of the center of the rock. A thong made from animal hide or plant fibers twisted into rope was tied around the groove. With this weapon in hand, a hunter could climb a tree and wait for his prey to pass below him. When some small game was in sight, he could stun the animal by throwing the rock at it. If he missed, he could pull the rock back up by its rope and try again.

The earliest yo-yos to be used as toys were carved from lignium vitae, meaning "wood of life," or made from the horn of the caribou or water buffalo. These first yo-yos were carved in the shape of a disc. A groove was made in the disc, and some string was knotted around the slim groove. The yo-yo was then played with by

Old "Duncan" wooden yo-yos: (bottom row) the Jewel, Butterfly, and Satellite; (middle) oversized wooden yo-yo awarded as a special prize; and (top row) Tournament and Butterfly have become collector's items.

The only difference between today's replacement strings and those of yesteryear is the price.

allowing the disc to spin toward the ground and the string to unwind and wind up again.

Later yo-yos were made with two discs joined by an axle, and more precious materials such as ivory, silver or gold were sometime incorporated.

In the United States yo-yos like the ones Pedro Flores made were originally hand-carved from one piece of wood. From the early thirties through the fifties, most American yo-yos were manufactured from "selected northern hard maple" and lacquered in assorted colors with distinctive, contrasting stripes. The strings were made of the finest Egyptian fibers. Two twisted strings with a loop at the bottom slipped around the axle of the yo-

22

yo instead of being knotted or attached to the axle.

By the end of the sixties most of the yo-yos made in this country were being manufactured of high-impact plastics, using the injection molding process. To produce the "Duncan" Professional model, for example, plastic chips are melted down and the liquid plastic is injected into molds the shape of yo-yo halves, 16 at a time.

When the yo-yo halves cool down, they are removed from the molds and the rough edges of the yo-yo sides are smoothed. Next, the sides are placed on a conveyer belt. As they move down the belt, a steel axle is pounded into one side of the yo-yo by hand. The other half of the yo-yo is placed on top, and a rivet or pin is inserted to hold the two halves together.

Continuing down the conveyer belt, the rivet is closed, and the two halves of the yo-yo are pressed together. Next, the "Duncan" label is affixed on both sides, and two clear plastic lenses are pressed

Some of today's line of plastic "Duncans," such as the Jewel, Butterfly, and Satellite, still retain the old names.

into place to enclose the label. Finally, the strings are slipped on and wound about the yo-yo axle with the help of a winding machine. The "Duncan" Professionals are then packaged, ready to be shipped to toy distributors all over the United States.

The slim-line professional is considered the yo-yo of the champions because its axle is especially designed for less string wear and quicker reaction to tricks. Other yo-yos manufactured by the Duncan Toy Division of Flambeau include: the Lil' Champ, with a single, anchored string for the smaller set to learn to yo-yo; the Special and Imperial, molded from high-quality plastic in assorted colors; the Butterfly that's great for string tricks; the Satellite, a butterfly yo-yo with a battery-powered bulb that lights up when you play with it; the Duncan Brands, with authentic Western brands stamped into the simulated wooden yo-yo; and the Jewel, with a pretend crystal, ruby, emerald, sapphire, or amethyst set into a black or white yo-yo. The comic-strip characters Batman, Robin, and Superman are featured on the "Duncan" Super Heroes yo-yos.

Besides their Be-a-Sport yo-yos shaped like sports equipment, "Festival" also manufactures the Little Zapper and Big Zapper, two wooden yo-yos for those still

"Festival's" wooden Big and Little Zapper. (Courtesy of Union Wadding Company.)

nostalgic for the old wooden Cheerio, the forerunner of the Zapper. The Dragonfly is the "Festival" version of the "Duncan" Butterfly.

A smaller yo-yo company, Royal, in Long Island, New York, owned by another Filipino and former "Duncan" demonstrator, Joe Rodavan, produces the Monarch, a plastic yo-yo with a metal axle much like the "Duncan" Imperial. Sayco's yo-yos are plastic with wooden axles. For a yo-yo that sleeps like the good old maple ones, Tom Kuhn has returned to making an all wooden model. He hand-turns his yo-yos on a lathe from one solid piece of hardwood. Some people, such as Gus Somera, "Duncan Pro," believe todays plastic yo-yos are the best; but then there are the Tom Kuhns who like nothing better than the feel of a wooden yo-yo in their palm.

Portrait of the old wooden Cheerio.

Tom Kuhn transforms a solid block of wood into a finished "No Jive" in his home workshop.

3
How Yo-Yos Work

In the chapter "A Yo-Yo Going Down, a Mad Squirrel Coming Up" from *Stop Time,* Frank Conroy describes how his yo-yo worked. "The string was not attached to the shank, but looped over it in such a way as to allow the wooden part to spin freely on its own axis. The gyroscopic effect thus created kept the yo-yo stable in all attitudes."

If the yo-yo were dropped the full length of its string without spinning, the two strings that are twisted together around the yo-yo shaft would unravel.

But this does not happen when the yo-yo is spinning because it is a simple gyroscope. The gyroscopic action resists the unwinding of the strings and keeps the yo-yo steady.

When the yo-yo is given an upward pull, it creates a force against the string and winds the string up upon itself. This action is best demonstrated in the yo-yo trick *Skyrocket.* After the yo-yo is thrown down toward the floor and it "sleeps" at the end of the string, the loop on the other end of the string is removed from the

Berkeley kids look on with wonder as Helane Zeiger, "Yo-Yo Pro," captures them with Spider Web.

finger. The yo-yo is held between the thumb and the second finger by the loop. Then it is released from the fingers and tossed up into the air. As the yo-yo shoots several feet up, the string winds itself up.

To Frank Conroy, "The greatest pleasure in yo-yoing was . . . watching the dramatization of simple physical laws, and realizing they would never fail if a trick was done correctly. The geometric purity of it! The string wasn't just a string, it was a tool in the enactment of theorems. It was a line, and idea. And the top was an entirely different sort of idea, a gyroscope, capable of storing energy and interacting with line."

WORLD ON A STRING

4

How to Care for Your Yo-Yo and Its String

Getting Your Yo-Yo Ready

1. Check to make sure the string of your yo-yo is the right length for you. Place the yo-yo between your feet. While holding it with your feet, pull up on the string as far as it will go. The proper length for you will be where the string reaches your waistline. Cut the string at that point.

Checking the length of the string.

2. Make a loop at the top of your yo-yo string. Make a slipknot loop by pulling part of the long end of the string through the loop.

Slipknot loop.

3. Place the slipknot over your middle finger.

Place slipknot over middle finger.

4. If you are using a new yo-yo or new string, spin the yo-yo to the right to tighten the string. Don't twist the string too tight. There should be some space in the loop around the axle.

5. If your yo-yo string is too tight and it's not "sleeping' long enough, spin the yo-yo to the left to loosen the string. That will make the yo-yo sleep longer.

Keeping Your Yo-Yo in Working Order

1. If your yo-yo string develops knots and gets tangled in the yo-yo, or becomes worn, you can replace the yo-yo string without buying a new yo-yo.

2. Buy a package of replacement yo-yo strings. Change the string by unwinding the old string at the end of the yo-yo. By twisting the string at the base to the left, you will be able to slip the string off the axle and over one of the yo-yo halves.

3. You might have to remove part of the old string with a sharp tool. That may be done with a nail file, paper clip, or crochet hook. Whatever tool you use, be careful not to scratch the axle of your yo-yo. That can damage the yo-yo permanently. The slightest cut in the axle will wear out new strings in two or three spins.

4. Untwist the bottom of your new string and slip it over one of the yo-yo halves and onto the axle. Tighten up the string as you would for a new yo-yo. Make a slipknot loop at the top before beginning to do tricks.

5. Do not attempt to repair a broken string with a knot. The knot will slow down the action of the yo-yo and get caught on the axle.

Winding Your Yo-Yo

1. One way to wind up your yo-yo string when it has become unwound is to lay out the string completely on the ground

Even winding your yo-yo is fun!

and roll the yo-yo up the string.

2. Another way to wind up the yo-yo is to wind the string around the yo-yo. Start by winding the string slowly. That will prevent the loop from continually slipping around the axle. When some string is wound up, continue to wind more quickly until all the string is wound around the yo-yo.

3. A more advanced way of winding the yo-yo is to place the string between your second and third fingers, with these fingers curving around the top of the yo-yo. Using the two fingers, spin the yo-yo toward you while pulling up on the yo-yo string with the other hand. This motion will cause the yo-yo to climb up the string, but the method requires practice.

Some Tips from the Pros

1. It is time to change your yo-yo string when it looks gray or worn out.

2. To make your yo-yo spin longer, rub a little candle wax or "Duncan" yo-yo wax (sold with replacement string) along the top four inches of the string, working from the loop down. To much wax will cause the yo-yo string to slip, so apply just a bit.

3. Don't get discouraged when learning a new trick. It takes a lot of practice and patience to learn each one.

4. Enjoy your yo-yo, but make sure nobody is close to you when you perform a trick. A yo-yo in the mouth can be a "jawbreaker"!

5

How to Do the Basic "Duncan" Tournament Tricks

Now that your yo-yo is ready and in good working order, you can teach yourself how to do any of the yo-yo tricks described in this book. Follow these instructions, practice a lot, and you can become the yo-yo champion of your neighborhood—or even a "Duncan Professional"! The first 10 tricks are described in the order of their difficulty. They are known as the basic "Duncan" tournament tricks.

The Spinner

This is the easiest trick to perform but a very important one, as it is the beginning of many more difficult tricks. Loop the slipknot of your yo-yo string over your middle finger with the knot on the inside of the finger. Make sure all your string is wound up tight. Bend your arm and turn your wrist so that your palm is up. Hold the yo-yo in the palm of your hand, making

sure the string leads off from the top of
your yo-yo. Now you are ready to do *The
Spinner.*

The Spinner.

The Spinner.

to ten seconds (two to four for a beginner),
jerk your hand upward. This will make the
yo-yo rewind and come back up to your
palm. Turn your hand over and catch the
yo-yo with your palm down.

Practice making your yo-yo spin, or
"sleep" for a longer and longer time.
According to the *Guinness Book of World
Records,* the longest anyone has ever made
a yo-yo spin is 15 seconds. Try beating the
record! "Mister Yo-Yo," professional Bob
Rule, says that the yo-yo needs to spin 6 to
8 seconds to perform the most difficult of
tricks.

Flick your wrist downward, throwing
the yo-yo toward the ground. When the
yo-yo completely unwinds, allow it to
spin, or "sleep," for as long as you can. Be
careful not to let the spinning yo-yo hit
the ground. After it has spun for about five

Walking-the-Dog

If you can "sleep" your yo-yo, you can learn to "walk it." Make your yo-yo "sleep" as described. Then gently lower the yo-yo to the ground. Walk the yo-yo out in front of you as if you were walking a dog on a leash. Keep the string taut. A small upward jerk of your wrist will return the yo-yo to your hand.

The Creeper.

The Creeper

First do a "sleeper" and then, *The Creeper.* While the yo-yo is spinning, straighten your arm, bend your body a little, and lower the yo-yo to the ground. Allow the string to unwind and the yo-yo to "creep" out in front of you. When the yo-yo reaches the end of the string, give the yo-yo a slight pull and it will start creeping back. As the string winds up, kneel down and catch the yo-yo.

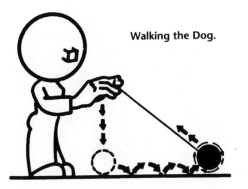

Walking the Dog.

Johnny-Round-the-Corner

Do a fast spinner. While the yo-yo is spinning, bring it around in back of your shoulder. Flip your wrist forward, and make the yo-yo hop over your shoulder. When the yo-yo is back in front of you, it will climb back up the string and into your hand. Here's a slightly harder version of the same trick. Again bring the yo-yo in back of your shoulder. This time reach down and tug on the string a few inches above the yo-yo. Once more the yo-yo will hop over your shoulder, come back in front of you, wind up the string, and return to your hand. Either way, "Johnny" will have come around the corner.

Skin-the-Cat

Throw a fast spinner. Slide the second finger of your free hand along the yo-yo string, a little bit down from the loop. At the same time, pull back on the string so that the string moves over your finger until you are about six inches away from the yo-yo. Next, gently flip the yo-yo out and over your hand so that it makes a loop inside your wrist. After you form the loop, it will return to your hand and you will have "skinned-the cat."

 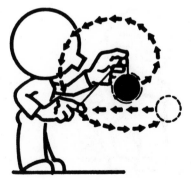

Rock-the-Baby

To do this trick, you "sleep" the baby before you rock him. So, make your yo-yo "sleep." About one-third of the way down from the yo-yo loop, drape the string over the fingers of your free hand. Next, about two-thirds down, drape the string over the fingers of your other hand. Drop your hand down, and open up your fingers to widen the cradle into the shape of a triangle. Lower your hand with the triangle on it, and allow the yo-yo to swing back and forth through the triangle two or three times. To make the yo-yo come back to your hand, swing it out in front of you and toward the floor. At the same time, let go of the cradle. The yo-yo then will climb back up the string. Practice forming your triangle and swinging the yo-yo through it with your string unwound.

Rock the Baby.

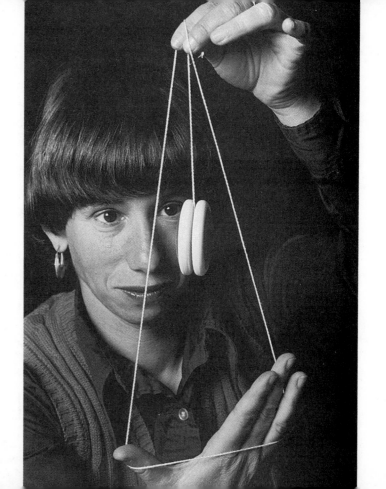

Sleeping Beauty

To begin this trick, make a muscle with your yo-yo hand. With your arm in this position, throw the yo-yo across your body to the right (if you are left-handed) or to the left (if your are right-handed) so that the yo-yo is on its side. While the yo-yo is spinning horizontally, pick up the string with your thumb and second finger at a point about two-thirds of the way down toward the yo-yo. To return the yo-yo to your hand, let go of the string you are holding with your fingers, and give it a sharp jerk with your other hand.

When you have learned *Sleeping Beauty*, you can use this trick to loosen the yo-yo string if you are right-handed or tighten the yo-yo string if you are left-handed. Throwing the yo-yo across your body to the right while it is spinning horizontally tightens the string. Throwing it to the left while it is spinning horizontally loosens the string.

Three-Leaf-Clover

Throw the yo-yo out in front of you, but slightly upward. This first motion is known as *Forward Pass.* As the yo-yo comes back toward you, flick your wrist inward and throw the yo-yo out directly in front of you again, making a loop and one of the clovers. When the yo-yo comes back to you a second time, flick your wrist so that the yo-yo goes inside your arm and moves downward toward the floor; that's the stem of your clover. Then jerk your wrist to make the yo-yo come back up to your hand.

Loop-the-Loop

Again throw the yo-yo out in front of you as in the *Three-Leaf-Clover*. As the yo-yo comes back toward you, let it go inside your arm, and snap your wrist outward again, making a loop. Keep your arm straight out in front of you, and continue as many times as you can to flick your wrist outward as the yo-yo comes back toward you. Try to throw the yo-yo out at a slight angle, as if you were facing a giant clock and throwing it toward an imaginary one o'clock if you're right-handed or eleven o'clock if you're left-handed.

Remember to make the loops inside your arm. During a yo-yo contest, this trick is often used to break a tie. The person who does the most loops is the winner. If you are left-handed, start with a very loose string because the yo-yo string will get tighter with every loop you make. If you are right-handed, tighten up your string because it will loosen as you continue to do more loops. Tony Flor holds the world's record for doing the most consecutive loops. On August 23, 1975, he did 7,531 loops. How many can you do?

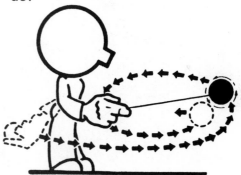

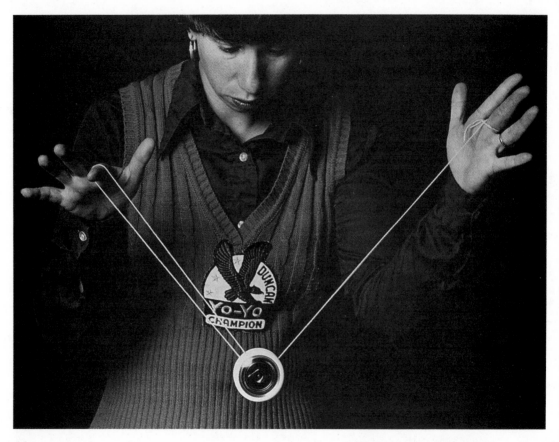

WORLD ON A STRING

Man on the Flying Trapeze

Begin this trick by throwing the yo-yo across your body as in *The Breakaway*. When the yo-yo reaches the end of the string, place your second finger about three inches from the yo-yo. Flip the yo-yo over so that it lands on the string. With the loop you've just made and your second finger, slide the yo-yo back and forth on the string and watch it do a balancing act!

Flip the yo-yo upward with both hands, slip your finger out of the loop, and the yo-yo will return to your hand.

When you have learned to do all 10 of the basic tournament tricks, you will be ready to enter a yo-yo contest—and you also will want to learn some more tricks. The intermediate tricks are a bit more difficult and will present a challenge for those who have mastered the beginning tricks.

6

Intermediate Tricks

Texas Cowboy ropes in the attention of a Berkeley, California audience.

Forward Pass

Start this trick with your yo-yo at your side and your hand palm down, with the string running clockwise from your finger. Swing your arm slightly in back of you; then swing it in front and up. Let go of the yo-yo at the same time, and throw it out in front of you. Catch the yo-yo with your palm up when the yo-yo returns to your hand.

The Breakaway

Palm the yo-yo in your hand with the string winding clockwise from the loop of the yo-yo. Now make a muscle with the arm that is holding the yo-yo. With your arm in this position, swiftly throw the yo-yo down and across your body from right to left. (If you're left-handed, throw it from left to right.) When the yo-yo reaches the end of the string, it will hesitate in midair for a few seconds. Then the yo-yo will snap back into your hand.

The Buzz Saw

This trick is done exactly the way you do *Walking-the-Dog.* But before you begin this trick, put a few pieces of paper, a newspaper, or a soft-covered book on the floor, Instead of walking the yo-yo across the floor, lower it to the paper. When the yo-yo touches the paper, it will make a sound like a buzz saw!

Around-the-World

Do this trick outdoors of in a large space as your yo-yo needs lots of room to travel "around the world." Make sure the area you select is clear of people. With the string leading off from the top of the yo-yo, throw it out in front of you as if you were doing *Forward Pass.* Then move your arm upward and behind you while the yo-yo continues its circle in back of you. The yo-yo string should be completely unwound as it makes its journey. The yo-yo will make a 360° arc and pass in front of you again.

When the yo-yo is out in front, you can pull it back into your hand and catch it. Or you can try letting the yo-yo go "around the world" two or three times before returning it to your hand.

Instead of going "around the world" along a line of longitude, try circling the globe along a line of latitude. Hold the yo-yo on its side with the strings leading off from the top. Bend your arm, and throw the yo-yo out as if you were a discus thrower. Make sure the yo-yo string is completely unwound as the yo-yo makes a full circle around your head. When the yo-yo comes back in front of you, jerk the string so that it will return to your hand.

Over-the-Falls

With the yo-yo string leading off from the top, throw it out in front of you as if you were doing *Forward Pass*. Then jerk the yo-yo back in when it is at the end of the string. But instead of catching it, flip your wrist so that the yo-yo goes inside your arm and moves downward toward the floor to make the "falls." Jerk your wrist upward, and the yo-yo will return to your hand.

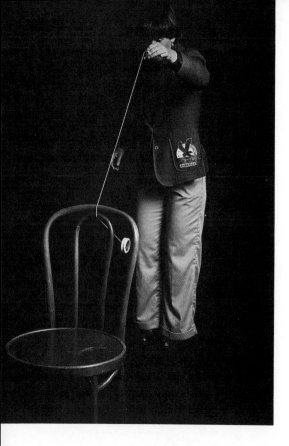

The Elephant's Trunk

Place an open-backed chair about two feet in front of you with its back facing toward you. Then throw a fast spinner and flip your yo-yo out and over the back of the chair. To create an "elephant's trunk," allow the yo-yo to dangle over the back of the chair as it continues to spin. Jerk the string back slightly to return the yo-yo to your hand.

The Dog Bite

This trick, as its name implies, is somewhat more dangerous! Begin with a fast spinner. Spread your legs about two feet apart, and let the yo-yo swing through them like a pendulum. When the yo-yo is behind your legs, jerk the string quickly so that the groove of the yo-yo catches on the back of your pants. If you're lucky, the yo-yo will appear to "bite" your leg.

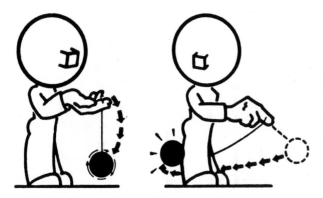

Hop the Fence

Throw a gentle spinner. As the yo-yo comes back up the string, curve your wrist. A gentle snap of the wrist in this position will make the yo-yo hop over your hand and travel downward again. Try making the yo-yo *Hop the Fence* several times!

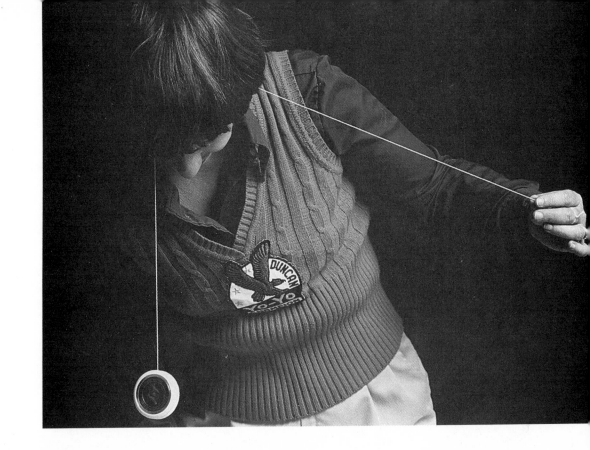

WORLD ON A STRING

The Guillotine

This trick is a variation of *Johnny-Round-the-Corner.* Instead of bringing the yo-yo in back of your shoulder, while it's spinning, bring it around your neck. Tug on the string the way you would for *Johnny-Round-the-Corner,* and the yo-yo will hop around your neck, down in front of you, and back up to your hand. Then you'll understand why it's called *The Guillotine*!

Walk-the-Dog and Jump Him Through a Hoop

Now that you've learned how to walk your dog, you can also teach him a trick! Start with a spinner. Instead of walking the dog out in front of you, bring the yo-yo behind your legs, and walk your yo-yo in between them. Put the hand with the yo-yo loop on your hip. Tug on the string as if you were doing *Johnny-Round-the-Corner.* Your smart dog will jump up behind you, through the hoop, over your arm, and down in front of you. Then he will come right back to your hand as a good dog should.

Flying Saucer

Start this trick by doing *Sleeping Beauty*. While the yo-yo is spinning on its side and you are holding the string between your thumb and second finger, make a muscle with your arm and move it out to your side. Let go of the string, and with your yo-yo hand, throw the yo-yo across your body and to the other side. While in a horizontal position, the yo-yo will orbit out and back to your hand like a flying saucer.

The Rattlesnake

This trick is another variation of *Sleeping Beauty*, except that the yo-yo is thrown on the opposite side. Throw the yo-yo down and sideways so that it spins at an angle. The yo-yo string will curl horizontally like a snake. Allow the twisting string to touch your pants or dress. The string will vibrate against the material and not only look like a snake but sound like the rattle of a rattlesnake!

60

Pickpocket

Here's a very novel trick that requires an assistant. Ask a friend to stand in front of you, a little farther away than the length of your yo-yo string. Let your arm rest naturally at your side. Then throw your yo-yo out in front of you, palm down, as if you were doing *Forward Pass*. But instead of catching it when the yo-yo returns, curve your wrist and snap the yo-yo slightly upward and out again in the direction of your friend's awaiting pocket. With enough practice and a little luck, you will be able to flip it into the pocket!

INTERMEDIATE TRICKS

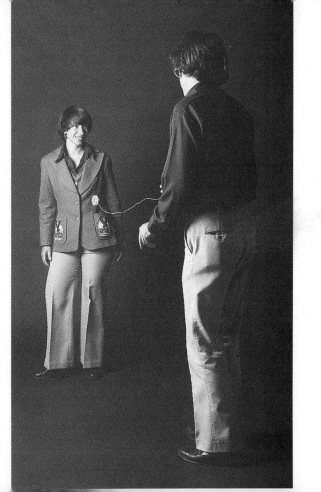

Bank Deposit

This is another way to deposit a yo-yo in a pocket, this time your own. Throw a spinner slightly out in front of you instead of straight down. As the yo-yo nears the ground, spread your legs and allow the yo-yo to swing between them and upward behind you. The yo-yo's own momentum will make it curve up and drop right into your side pocket!

62

Pinwheel

Do a fast spinner. Grasp the string about eight inches from the yo-yo with the thumb and second finger of your free hand. Extend the yo-yo out to the side, and whirl the string in a circle with your two fingers. This causes a "pinwheel" effect. Remove your fingers from the string before the spin runs out, and the yo-yo will return to your hand.

Monkey Climbing the String

After you've thrown a fast spinner, drape the string over your second finger and slip it into the front groove of the yo-yo. With the string in this position, pull the hand with the yo-yo loop down and your second finger up, and watch your "monkey" climb up the string right to the top! Slip your second finger out of the string, and your "monkey" will climb down and back into your hand! (Slip your finger out about an inch from the top.)

Pinwheel.

Monkey Climbing the String.

Thread the Needle

Throw a fast spinner. Drape the string over your second finger and away from your body. Now you will have two strings. Thread one string through the groove of the yo-yo while it is spinning. With your second finger between the strings, move your arm slightly outward and you will be "threading a needle." To return the yo-yo to your hand, slip your finger out of the loop you have just formed.

The Elevator

Start with a spinner. Now loop the string over your second finger, and slip it into the back groove of the yo-yo. With the string in this position, slowly pull the hand with the yo-yo loop down and your second finger up. Watch the elevator shoot up to the top floor! Coming down, you can call out the floors like an elevator operator: "Fourth floor, third, second, first, basement, ladies' lingerie!"

Shotgun

This trick is a variation of *Thread the Needle*. Hold another yo-yo in your free hand. Do *Thread the Needle*. When the yo-yo gets to the top of the string, let it hit the other yo-yo. This will produce a "pop" sound like a shotgun!

WORLD ON A STRING

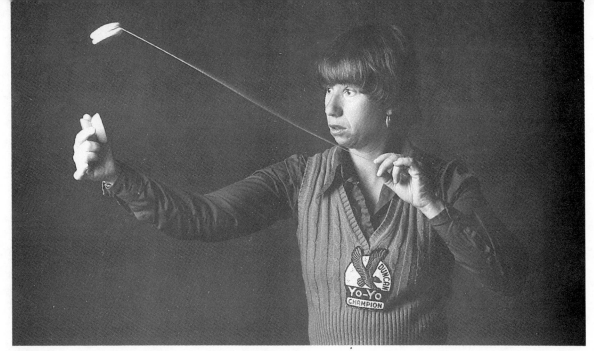

Shotgun.

Machine Gun

This is a fun trick that's best performed when there aren't any cops around or you'll be *Behind Bars!* (See next trick.) Throw a fast spinner. While the yo-yo is spinning, place your second finger behind the yo-yo string, about six inches down from the loop. Drape the yo-yo over your second finger while bringing the other hand out in front of the second finger. Then lower the hand out in front to six inches below the second finger. Now drape the yo-yo string over the middle finger of the hand with the loop on it. Now move your second finger out in front. Use it to aim your machine gun, and you can "rat-tat-tat" at your favorite pretend target by doing *Walking-the-Dog* on a table or chair at the same time. Slip your second finger out from between the two strings, and jerk the yo-yo up to return it to your hand.

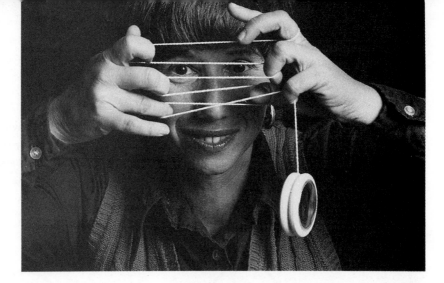

Behind Bars

If you should shoot someone with your *Machine Gun,* you might end up *Behind Bars.* Here's how to do it. "Sleep" your yo-yo. Using your second finger, grab the yo-yo string about six inches down from the loop. With this finger, pull the string out to the side. Now grab the string another six inches down with the fourth finger of the hand with the loop on it. Pull the string to the other side. Using the middle finger of the opposite hand, grab the string another six inches down, and pull the string to the side. Do this once more with the pinkie of the hand with the loop. Now you will have made four bars. Lift all the horizontal strings in front of your face, and you will be *Behind Bars!*

Through the Subway

This trick is performed by doing *Around-the-World* in reverse. Hold the yo-yo in your hand, with your palm facing upward as if you were getting ready to do *The Spinner*. Throw the yo-yo toward the ground with a quick downward snap and with the back of the hand following through behind you. Rotate your arm in the opposite direction from the way you would move it for *Around-the-World*. The yo-yo will travel in back of you first, then over your head and in front of you. When the yo-yo has completed one revolution from back to front, swing it between your legs. Quickly pull on the string after the yo-yo has passed through your legs, as if you were completing *The Creeper*, and it will return to your hand.

Texas Cowboy

Throw a spinner across your body. Let the yo-yo spin sideways about a foot from the floor, and allow it to travel in a circle. As the yo-yo approaches your left leg, lift it and allow the yo-yo to pass under your left foot. Put your left foot down, and lift up your right foot as the yo-yo approaches it. Let the yo-yo pass under your right foot and continue out in front of you. Now jerk the string and return the yo-yo to your hand. That's ropin' 'em cowboy!

Home Run

If you can be a cowboy or cowgirl with a yo-yo, you also can be a baseball player. See how many bases you can make with your yo-yo. Pretend you're home plate. A few inches from your right foot is first. Second base is about a foot in front of you, and third is about a foot from second base. Then you're back at home plate.

Now run the bases with your yo-yo. Throw a fast spinner, and move it down to first base at an angle. With the yo-yo still spinning on its side, try for second, then third, and, finally all the way home! The yo-yo will be moving in a semicircle in front of you. With a very fast spinner, it is possible to walk the yo-yo in a full circle through all the bases to make a *Home Run!*

72

Rounding Second Base!

Spaghetti

After learning all these tricks, you might get a little hungry. So try eating *Spaghetti!* Throw a fast spinner. Drape the yo-yo string over your second finger, about four fingers down from the loop. Now drape the string over the top of the second finger of your other hand four inches down from the first finger. Continue to wrap the yo-yo string around these two fingers as if you were twirling spaghetti around a fork. When you almost run out of string, bring the whole wrapped wad to your mouth and pretend to eat it. Mmm, Mmm good! Let go of all the string, make all gone with your spaghetti, and the yo-yo will pop into your hand!

Reach-for-the-Moon

Throw the yo-yo upward and out in front of you as if you were starting to do *Three-Leaf-Clover*. As the yo-yo heads back to your hand, curve your wrist and snap it in and up. This action of your wrist will shoot the yo-yo a little in back of you and upward again. When the yo-yo travels back toward your hand and descends, snap your wrist as if you were doing *Loop-the-Loop*. This will make the yo-yo move out in front of you again. When the yo-yo descends and comes back to your hand a third time, you can either catch it or *Reach-for-the-Moon* again by repeating the above directions!

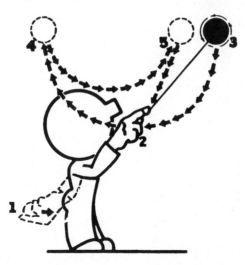

The Coin Trick

This amazing trick, perfected by Tom McCoy, "Duncan Pro," can be learned by the amateur. What it calls for is precision control of *Loop-the-Loop.* So practice this trick until you can do a series of loops with perfect control. Then take a coin and prop it up on something. Practice knocking the coin off your prop with the yo-yo while doing *Loop-the-Loop.* When you have total control of the yo-yo, you are ready to place the coin on top of a friend's ear! After doing a few loops to get the range, you should be able gently to graze the top of your friend's ear with the yo-yo and knock the coin off! Here's a penny for Good Luck!

7
Advanced Tricks

Texas Star amazes Helane Zeiger as well as her audience.

The following tricks are more difficult and will take practice and patience to perfect. The hours spent learning them, however, will bring you much enjoyment. Now that you've mastered all the intermediate tricks and are ready for the challenge of the more intricate string tricks, you can give yourself a star. Here's how you do it.

Texas Star

Throw a really fast spinner. Using your free hand, place the inside of your thumb against the yo-yo string about six inches down from the top. With your yo-yo hand, drape the string across the top of your thumb and pull the string so that it is in front of your chest and in a horizontal position. Now, with the fourth finger of the hand with the loop, grab the outside of the string another six inches down. Pull the string so that it is horizontal to the first string. Place the outside of the second finger of your free hand against the yo-yo string another six inches down. Pull the string so that it is horizontal to the first string. Place the outside of the second finger of your free hand against the yo-yo string another six inches down. Then lift this portion of the string above and in front of the two horizontal strings.

You now will notice that you have formed three points of the star. Using the thumb of the hand with the loop, pull the dangling string through the horizontal strings. This will give you the fourth point. To make the last point of the star, use the outside of the second finger of the hand with the loop to lift the string up. Rotate your hands slightly so that the remaining string hangs down from the top center point. To end this dazzling trick, remove your fingers from the points of the star. Let the string go down, and the yo-yo will come back up to your hand.

At first, practice making the star with the string slack and without spinning your yo-yo. When you can create a star with the yo-yo string, try doing it while the yo-yo is spinning. If you can make a star while the yo-yo is spinning, you deserve it!

Shooting Star

Once you have perfected *Texas Star*, you can turn it into a "shooting star"! Here's how. Make a *Texas Star*. With the remaining string hanging down from the top center point, circle the star one or two times by swinging the yo-yo toward you and over the top of the star. As the yo-yo comes toward you on the last swing, shoot out all the string as if you were doing *Forward Pass.* Be ready to catch the yo-yo as it shoots back toward you.

Third Dimension

Like *Shooting Star,* this trick shoots out! (Some "Pros" call it *Shoot the Teacher.*) Start by throwing a really good spinner. About one-third down the yo-yo string, grab the string with the four fingers of your free hand. Now grab it again with the thumb and second finger of your yo-yo hand. With the remaining string hanging down from where you have grabbed it with your two fingers, circle the two strings at that point. As in *Shooting Star,* circle the strings by swinging the yo-yo toward you and over the top one or two times. As the yo-yo comes toward you on the last circle, shoot out all the string into the *Third Dimension!* Be ready to catch the yo-yo as it shoots back to you.

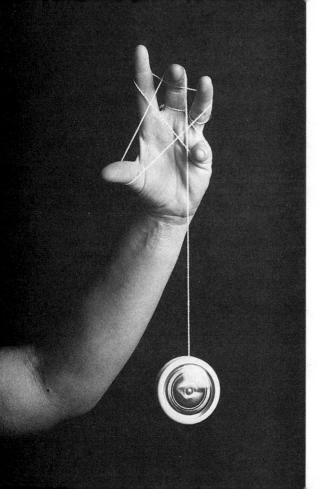

One-Handed Star

Practice this string-formation trick without spinning the yo-yo. For this trick you will be using only the fingers on the hand with the yo-yo loop. Place the outside of your pinky finger against the inside of the string, about two or three inches down from the loop. Lift the string upward with your pinky. Then reach down another three inches, and with your second finger, go around the string, looping the string around it. Lift the string and the second finger up.

Now put your fourth finger against the inside of the string another three inches down, and lift the string up. With your thumb another three inches down the string, go around the string in the same way you looped the string around your second finger. Put your middle finger against the inside of the string just as you did your fourth finger, and lift the string up. Adjust your fingers so that you can see the formation of a baby star. Now try to do it while the yo-yo is spinning!

Bow-Tie

Another fun, picture-string trick is *Bow-Tie*. Start by throwing a spinner. About four inches down from the loop, drape the string over the thumb, second, and third finger of your free hand. About four inches down, drape the string over the thumb, second, and third finger of your yo-yo hand. Now put a twist in the string with your free hand, and pull down on the loop you've made around these fingers. With the thumb and second finger of this hand, pull the string down through the loop another few inches. Point you thumb, second, and third finger out, and stretch out those fingers to form a triangle and one-half of the "bow-tie." Now stretch out the fingers of your other hand, and bring your thumb down so that these fingers are in the same position as the fingers of your other hand. Now you will have a *Bow-Tie*. If you flap each side of the *Bow-Tie*, you can change it into a *Butterfly*.

ADVANCED TRICKS

The Motorcycle

You can ride a *Motorcycle* in much the same way you make a *Bow-Tie*. Drape the string over the thumb, second, and third fingers of both hands the same way you did for *Bow-Tie*. Now put a twist in the string with your free hand, and pull the loop you've made around these fingers down. Reach for the string through the loop with only your thumb. Hook your thumb around the string, and pull it through the loop. Now hold the other loop with just your thumb. You will now have a loop around each thumb. Hold the strings in this position, lower the yo-yo to the floor. You can now "vroom-vroom" your *Motorcycle* by *Walking-the-Dog* between your legs.

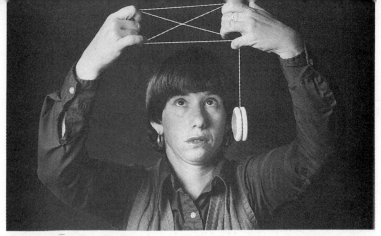

Confederate Flag

Practice this string-formation trick at first without spinning the yo-yo. Grab the yo-yo string with four fingers of your free hand about four inches down form the loop. Now grab the string another four inches down with the second, third, and fourth fingers of your other hand. Pull the strings tight across so that you have formed a triangle. Now reach down with the triangle and again grab the string with the four fingers at the base of the triangle. Pull the strings tight across. You will notice that you have formed a straight line and an "x." With the free pinky of your hand with the yo-yo loop, pick up the string another four inches down and bring it across. This string will form the bottom of a *Confederate Flag*. Once you have learned this string configuration, you can make a *Confederate Flag* while the yo-yo is spinning—and why not whistle "Dixie" at the same time!

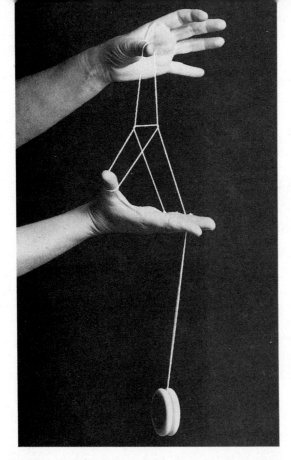

Eiffel Tower.

Eiffel Tower and "Y" is for Yo-Yo

Practice the formation of this trick without spinning the yo-yo. Begin by draping the string over the thumb and second finger of your free hand. Pull the string down and over these fingers. About three or four inches down from your thumb and second finger, place the outside of your thumb on the hand with the loop against the outside of the string. Put a twist in the string, and pull the twisted loop down over your thumb.

Now grab the single yo-yo string with your thumb and second finger, and pull the string through the loop. Let go of the twisted loop, and allow it to slide down the string. Slip the single string between

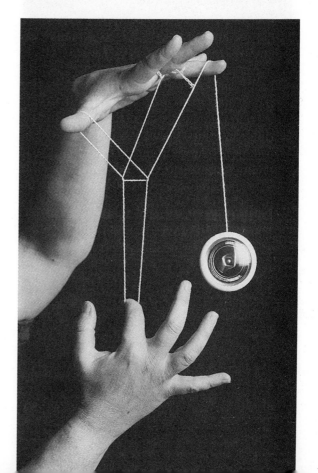

"Y" is for Yo-Yo.

the second and middle finger of the hand with the loop. Adjust your fingers so that the strings are taut and look like a tower.

If you turn the tower upside-down, you will discover another string-formation trick. The upside-down tower looks like a "Y." Tell your friends the *"Y"* is for Yo-Yo.

Once you can form the tower and the "Y" with a dead yo-yo, try doing it while the yo-yo is spinning. If you throw the spinner to the side so that one side of the yo-yo faces front before you form the "Y," the round yo-yo will fall into place next to the "Y" and be the "O" in "YO"!

ADVANCED TRICKS

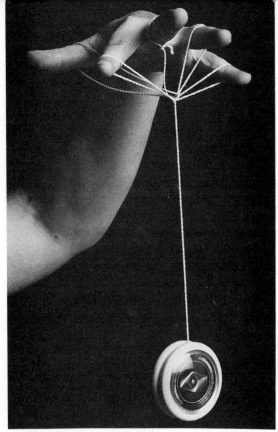

Spider Web 1.

Spider Web

No two spider webs are exactly alike. Here's how to do two different ones.

Spider Web 1

Start by draping the string over all the fingers of your free hand. Now make a twist in the string with these fingers. Using the thumb on your other hand, place the outside of the thumb against the front of the string below the twist. Lift the string with your thumb. Bring the triangle you have formed down, and with your thumb and second finger, pull the string through it. Drop the triangle.

Place the outside of your fourth finger against the back of the string, just below the new triangle you have formed. Lift the string up with your forth finger. Bring the triangle down, and pull the string through it. Drop the old triangle.

Bring the next triangle down, and lift the string with your pinky finger. Pull the string through this triangle. Place the new loop you have just made on your second finger (the only free finger). Pull the strings

WORLD ON A STRING

down so that they look like four loops coming out from a center. The yo-yo will hang down from this center point.

Practice making the web without spinning the yo-yo. Keep the loops close to the end of your fingers for a better web. When you have learned to form the web, practice it with a *Spinner*. To end the trick, simply remove your fingers from the loops, and the yo-yo will come back up to your hand. If you should accidentally get a knot in your string, you can tell your friends that you caught a fly in your *Spider Web*.

Spider Web 2

Begin forming the web exactly as you would for *Spider Web 1*. After lifting the string with your fourth finger, pull the string through the triangle and bring the new triangle all the way down. You'll notice that you have formed a cradle. Swing the yo-yo through it and you will *Rock-the-Baby* in a *Spider Web*. End the trick by letting go of all the string around your fingers. The yo-yo will go down and then back up to your hand.

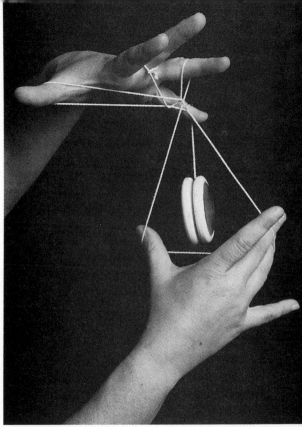

Spider Web 2.

Double or Nothing

Start this trick as if you were doing *Breakaway* by quickly throwing the yo-yo across your body from right to left or from left to right. As the yo-yo reaches the end of the string, place the second finger of your free hand on the yo-yo string about halfway down from the yo-yo. Allow the yo-yo to loop over this finger. The yo-yo will then travel in the direction of your other hand. As it completes its upward arc, catch the string again with your second finger. Loop the yo-yo around this finger before it travels downward and across again. Then let it loop once again around the second finger of your other hand. Now the yo-yo is ready to land on any of the horizontal strings in much the same way it drops onto the string in *Man on the Flying Trapeze.* Once you can do *Double or Nothing* with ease, go for a *Triple!*

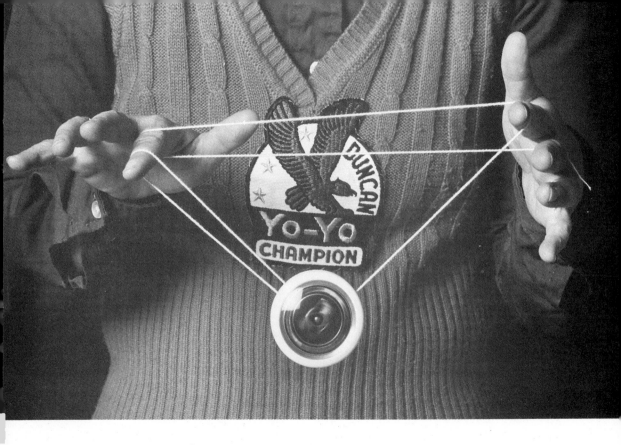

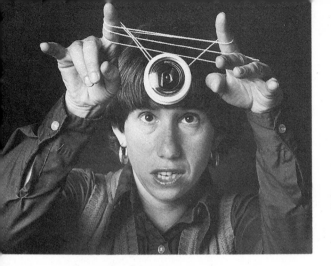

Triple or Nothing

Do *Double or Nothing,* but let the yo-yo string loop around your two extended fingers once more before the yo-yo lands on one of the strings. To complete either *Double or Triple or Nothing,* slip your fingers out of the loops after you've flipped the yo-yo slightly upward with both hands. Get ready to catch the yo-yo as it comes down.

Completing Double or Triple or Nothing.

Quadruple or Nothing!

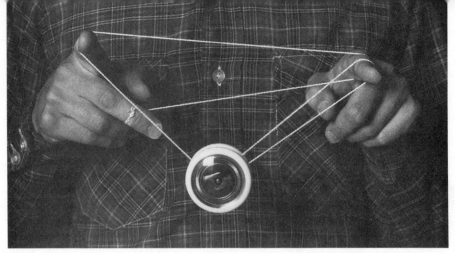

Roller Coaster

Ready for a real yo-yo thrill? Try learning the *Roller Coaster!* It's one of the hardest tricks! (Directions are written for right-handers; reverse directions if left handed.) Do *Double or Nothing.* Pull your right hand out of the string. Pull down on the string with your yo-yo hand so that the yo-yo rolls over your left index finger. Then, with your right index finger, push the yo-yo back toward you. You actually are doing a *Lindy Loop.* Reverse directions and do another one. Do as many *Lindy Loops* as you can, allowing for your spinner. End up in *Man on the Flying Trapeze.* With your right hand, pull the string over the top of your left index finger, and snap the yo-yo behind you as if you were doing a reverse *Forward Pass.* Get ready to catch the yo-yo as it comes back behind you. Did you keep the car on the roller coaster track for the whole trick? If not, try again!

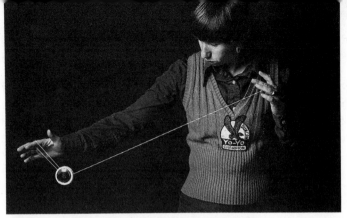

Man on the Flying
Trapeze reviewed.

Advanced Man on the Flying Trapeze Tricks

Several tricks described in this selection begin with *Man on the Flying Trapeze*. Let's review this trick. Start by doing the *Breakaway*. When the yo-yo reaches the end of the string and begins to spin in midair, place the second finger of your free hand about three inches down from the end of the string. The yo-yo will loop over this finger and land on the string. Let it straddle the string for a few seconds. Flip the yo-yo upward with both hands. Slip

your finger out of the loop. The yo-yo then will return to your hand. When you are able to do *Man on the Flying Trapeze* almost automatically, you're ready to do it in combination with the following tricks:

Man on the Flying Trapeze and Double or Nothing.

This trick is done by doing two tricks in rapid succession. Practice them separately until you're expert at both of them. Start by doing *Man on the Flying Trapeze*. Allow the yo-yo to stay on the string for only a couple of seconds. Then flip the yo-yo off the string. With the yo-yo string caught between your second and third finger, send the yo-yo moving across your body over the top of your second finger. As the yo-yo travels toward your other hand, loop it over your other second finger. Complete this trick by doing the rest of *Double or Nothing.*

Your timing is very important in executing this very difficult trick. You must move quickly through each step to finish both tricks before the spin of the yo-yo runs out. When you have mastered this intricate combination, you will astonish your friends as well as yourself!

Man on the Flying Trapeze and His Brother

Begin this trick by doing *Man on the Flying Trapeze.* Allow the yo-yo to stay on the string for just a few seconds. Next, flip it back off the string with your second finger. As the yo-yo flips back off the string, catch it between your thumb and second finger. With the string in this position, snap your wrist and send the yo-yo down across your body in the opposite direction. The yo-yo should be moving like a pendulum.

When the yo-yo reaches your other hand, extend your second finger and loop the yo-yo over it. The yo-yo should land on the string on the other side. To insure its landing, keep the string a little slack between your two hands, and try to make the yo-yo land on the outside string. To end this trick, flip the yo-yo back off the string and catch it again in your hand.

If you complete *Man on the Flying Trapeze* but miss landing his brother on the other side, just tell your friends you've done *Man on the Flying Trapeze and His Half Brother!* But if you learn to land his brother, try landing his sister by flipping the brother off the string and once again sending the yo-yo down and across your body. Again flip the yo-yo over your extended second finger and onto the string. Flip the sister off the string and up and back into your hand, or try for his *Mother-in-Law!*

Man on the Flying Trapeze and Rock-the-Baby

Here's how the yo-yo professionals *Rock-the-Baby!* First do *Man on the Flying Trapeze.* After the yo-yo lands on the string, slide it down about halfway. Open up the yo-yo strings and form the cradle by putting the rest of your fingers through the two strings and stretching them out. Now place the thumb of the hand with the loop on it behind the two strings about halfway down. Drape the two strings over the thumb, and pull the cradle down. Now your yo-yo baby should be in just the right position to rock in its cradle. Let the yo-yo swing through the strings a few times.

To finish, lift the cradle up, and remove all your fingers except the second. Lower your hand with the loop on it and remove the trapeze string. An upward jerk of your wrist will return the yo-yo to the starting point. For an even more spectacular ending, instead of returning the yo-yo to

Man on the Flying Trapeze and Rock-the-Baby.

your hand, place your second finger behind the yo-yo string. Pull back on the string with your other hand. Lift the yo-yo slightly upward with the second finger about two-thirds down the string from the loop. Then flick your wrist and do one *Loop-the-Loop.* You actually are finishing off with *Skin-the-Cat.* After the yo-yo comes back to you, you will have executed three different tricks: *Man on the Flying Trapeze, Rock-the-Baby,* and *Skin-the-Cat.* It's a show stopper!

Double Man on the Flying Trapeze

Make the daring young man on the flying trapeze do two flips forward and two flips backward with your yo-yo. First do *Man on the Flying Trapeze.* Place your second finger, as well as the two strings it is between, onto the trapeze string. At this point, slip the remaining string between your second and third fingers, and flip the yo-yo onto the single string again. Next, flip the yo-yo back off the string twice for the two backward flips. Then make the yo-yo return to your hand. You also can flip the yo-yo back off and down once. Flip the yo-yo upward with both hands before catching it.

98

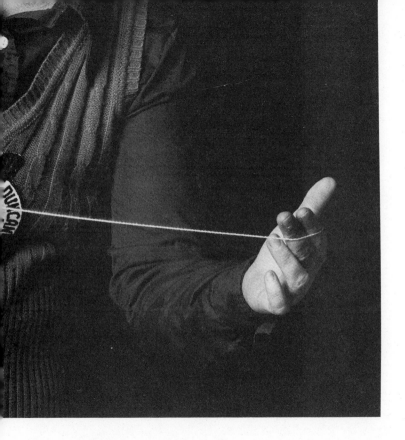

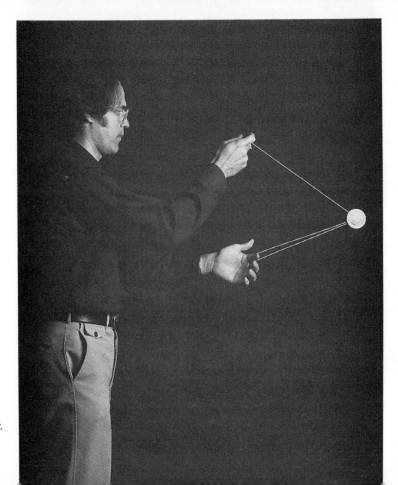

Bill deBoisblanc does Brain Twister.

Brain Twister

Begin this trick by throwing a really fast spinner. While the yo-yo is spinning, place the outside of the second finger of your free hand against the yo-yo string about halfway down. Pull the string over your second finger and down into the yo-yo grove nearest your body. Loop the string around the axle, and bring it around to the front groove of the yo-yo. You should have two strings in the back groove coming down from your second finger and one string in the front groove coming down from the loop on your middle finger. The yo-yo will be in the middle of the strings.

Now place the inside of your free second finger against the two back strings. Flip the yo-yo over this finger by moving the second finger in between the two strings, forward, then down, then around and up in a counter-clockwise circle. This motion is called a *Lindy Loop,* named after the famous aviator, Charles Lindberg, who flew the first plane non-stop and solo across the Atlantic Ocean.

You can flip the yo-yo over and do two or three *Lindy Loops* by repeating this circular action. To complete the trick, lower the hand with the loop after you have finished a circle and slip the string from the groove. The outside of your other second finger will still be touching the string. Pull the string over this finger. Flip the yo-yo up with the loop you've just made and end with a *Skin-the-Cat.*

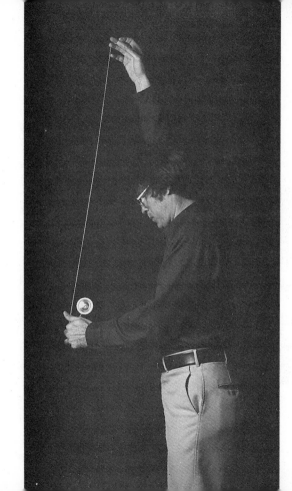

Brain Twister from the Bottom

Begin this variation of *Brain Twister* by again throwing a spinner. Run the outside of your second finger down the back of the string until it reaches the yo-yo. Flip the yo-yo onto the string, and pull up on the loop you've just made around your second finger. Again, your strings should be in the *Lindy Loop* position. Now continue to do *Brain Twister* as described in the preceding directions.

Brain Twister over the Top

This second variation starts with a spinner. While the yo-yo is spinning, run your free middle finger down the front of the yo-yo string. At the same time, pull the yo-yo string over your middle finger and down in front of the yo-yo. When your middle finger nears the top of the yo-yo, extend your second finger and flip the yo-yo over the top of your middle finger, around your second finger, and onto the yo-yo string. Lower the yo-yo until it is in the center of the string. You again will have two strings coming down from your second finger and in the back groove of the yo-yo and one string coming down from the loop on your middle finger. This string will be in the front groove. Now you are ready to continue the *Brain Twister* as you ordinarily would. (See directions for *Brain Twister*.)

Man on the Flying Trapeze and Brain Twister

This version of *Brain Twister* begins by first doing *Man on the Flying Trapeze.* Slide the yo-yo down to the center of the string. Once again you will find three strings in the *Lindy Loop* position. Once more place your free second finger against the two strings. Flip the yo-yo toward you with this finger. To end the trick, flip the yo-yo upward with both hands. Slip your second finger out of the loop and catch the yo-yo at this point. Or you can finish off with *Skin-the-Cat.* To really twist your brain, practice all four versions of *Brain Twister* until you're expert at doing all of them!

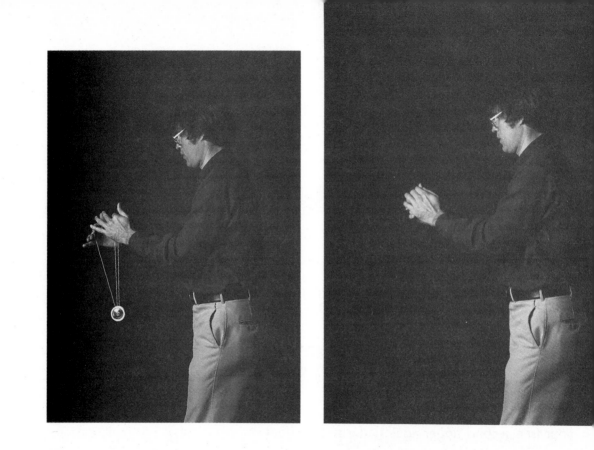

WORLD ON A STRING

Perpetual Motion, or Stop and Go

This is a nifty trick because after you've stopped the yo-yo, you make it go again. This is how you do it. First throw a good spinner. Then slip the string in the groove nearest you and around the axle just as if you were going to do *Brain Twister*. You will have a loop around your second finger and a single string leading down from the loop on your yo-yo hand. Let the yo-yo spin a couple of seconds in this position. Then jerk your hand upward and catch the yo-yo with the strings still in this position. Now the yo-yo has stopped spinning. To start it going again, bring the single string down and snap the yo-yo up by the loop around your second finger. This motion will cause the yo-yo to move upward and then back down to your hand.

Dizzy Baby

Have you ever seen a baby that won't settle down in the cradle? That's a dizzy baby! Here's how to make your yo-yo baby a dizzy one. Do *Rock-the-Baby* as you ordinarily would. Holding the portion of the string near the yo-yo between your thumb and second finger, swing the yo-yo toward you and through the cradle. Then swing it around one cradle string to the front, around the other cradle string, and back into the cradle through the back. To complete the trick, swing the yo-yo toward you again, around one cradle string and to the front, and around the other cradle string and into the cradle through the back. Let go of the cradle and the yo-yo will return to your hand. If the directions didn't get you dizzy, you will have done *Dizzy Baby!*

Rock-the-Baby and Throw it Out of Its Cradle

Want to know what to do with a baby that just won't sleep? First rock it, and then throw it out of its cradle. Here's how you do it. Do *Rock-the-Baby* as you ordinarily would. At the same time you are forming the cradle, grab the yo-yo string about three inches from the yo-yo with your thumb and middle finger. Swing the yo-yo through the cradle a couple of times with these fingers. As the yo-yo travels toward you on the last swing, throw it out of the cradle by looping it over the top of the cradle and then back over and into the cradle again. Drop the cradle strings and catch the yo-yo as it heads back up to your hand. That should put the baby to sleep!

Double Rock-the-Baby

To do this trick, form two cradles instead of one and rock the baby in a double cradle. Make the first cradle by draping

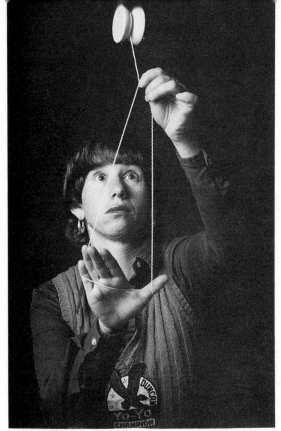

Rock-the-Baby and Throw It Out of Its Cradle.

WORLD ON A STRING

the string over the fingers of your free hand about one-fourth of the way down from the loop. Pull the string down in front of your other hand and extend the middle finger of the hand with the loop on it. Place the yo-yo string on the inside of your middle finger another one-fourth of the way down. Pull that string down with your other hand.

You will have two strings coming down from your middle finger. Open up your other fingers, and form your first cradle in the shape of a triangle. Drop your first cradle another one-fourth of the way down the string, and form your second cradle exactly the same way you formed the first. Stretch out your thumb and other fingers to open up both cradles at the same time. Your yo-yo will be in the right position to swing through them.

Rock the yo-yo back and forth through both triangles with your middle finger. Drop all the cradle strings, and the yo-yo will go down and back up into your hand. First practice forming the cradles without

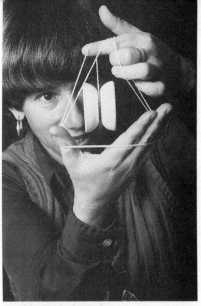

Double Rock-the-Baby.

spinning the yo-yo. When you are ready to try the trick, throw a really fast spinner. If there's enough spin left after you've rocked the baby through two triangles, try throwing the baby out of a double cradle by following the directions for the preceding trick!

Skyrocket

Throw a really fast spinner. While the yo-yo is "sleeping," slip the loop off your finger. As you hold the loop, quickly jerk your hand and let go of the yo-yo. This motion will send the yo-yo skyrocketing upward as it also climbs up the string. For a really fantastic finale to your yo-yo show, while the yo-yo is still in midair, open up the pocket of your jacket or pants with your free hand. Catch the yo-yo in your pocket when it comes down, and the show is over!

WORLD ON A STRING

8

Two-Handed Yo-Yo Tricks

The following tricks are very difficult to perform, and you should only attempt to learn them after you have mastered all the one-handed tricks. When you feel you are ready to yo-yo with two hands, start by learning to do *The Spinner* simultaneously with both hands. Then try doing double *Walking-the-Dog* and double *Creeper*. Get into the habit of holding a yo-yo in each hand. Soon you will be ready to learn two-handed *Loop-the-Loop*.

Double Creeper.

Two-Handed Loop-the-Loop

Start by practicing *Loop-the-Loop* with the yo-yo hand you don't ordinarily use. When you have attained enough skill with that hand, do *Loop-the-Loop* simultaneously with both hands.

Crisscross

Start by doing *Loop-the-Loop* simultaneously with both hands. When you have both yo-yos going together smoothly, make the strings cross as one yo-yo goes outward and the other is on its return journey.

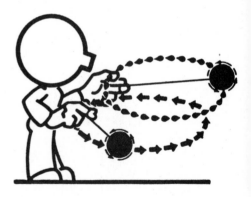

Crisscross.

Dan Volk does Crisscross.

Ride the Horse

Do *Loop-the-Loop* with one hand in front of you. At the same time, do *Hop the Fence* with the other hand behind you. With the yo-yos moving in opposite directions, it looks as though you're riding a horse!

Ride the Horse.

Punching the Bag

This is done by doing *Loop-the-Loop* with one hand and at the same time doing a reverse *Loop-the-Loop* with the other hand. These two opposing motions are extremely difficult to coordinate, so practice by moving one hand in a circular motion one way and moving the other hand in the opposite direction without actually sending the yo-yos in and out. Practice it until you can move your hands in different directions at the same time.

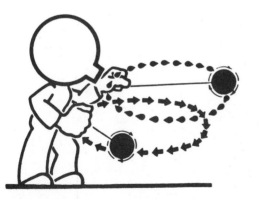

Milking the Cow

"Milk the cow" by doing *Hop the Fence* at the same time with both hands. Once you can do this with both yo-yos moving simultaneously in the same direction, make the trick look even more difficult by having one yo-yo go down while the other one is going up. Then, for an even more spectacular display of coordination, spread your legs apart and continue the up and down motion of both yo-yos between your legs.

WORLD ON A STRING

Loop-the-Loop and Reach-for-the-Moon

Do *Loop-the-Loop* with one hand. At the same time, do *Reach-for-the-Moon* with the other hand, keeping both yo-yos going. Keep your eyes on the yo-yo doing *Reach-for-the-Moon,* as even the most expert players will miss this trick and get a yo-yo in the eye!

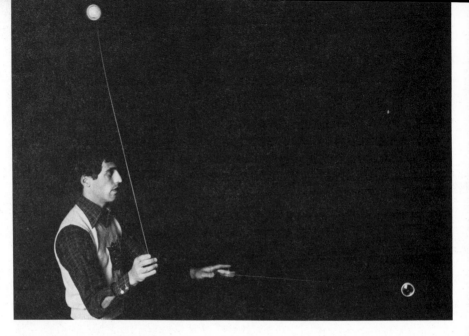

Loop-the-Loop and Around-the-World

Starting by doing *Loop-the-Loop* with both hands. While doing loops with one hand, send the yo-yo *Around-the-World* with the other. After you've done *Around-*the-World once, continue doing *Loop-the-Loop* with both hands. When you feel like it, send one or both of your yo-yos *Around-the-World* again and then back into *Loop-the-Loop*.

Two-Handed Reach-for-the-Moon

This trick is perhaps the most difficult of all the two-handed tricks. Practice doing *Reach-for-the-Moon* with the hand you don't ordinarily use until you can do it perfectly. Practice doing *Reach-for-the-Moon* with your yo-yo hand until you can do it without keeping your eye on the yo-yo. Then try doing this trick with both hands. See if you can do *Reach-for-the-Moon* two or three times with both hands simultaneously. When you can do this standing up, try doing *Two-Handed Reach-for-the-Moon* on your knees. Either standing or kneeling, you'll wish you had an extra pair of eyes in order to watch both yo-yos!

TWO HANDED YO-YO TRICKS

9

How to Run Your Own Yo-Yo Contest

The Duncan Yo-Yo Company originally created the rules and scoring for neighborhood yo-yo contests. They are as follows:

Rules

Each contestant will do any 10 different tricks.
1. If the performer misses on the first try, he is allowed one more chance for each trick.
2. Each contestant takes a turn doing a trick. This continues until everyone has completed 10 tricks.
3. If the string breaks during a trick, a second chance is allowed the contestant without penalty.
4. Each trick must end with yo-yo back in the player's hand and the string wound up in the yo-yo.

Scoring

1. 10 points given when the trick is done on first try.
2. 5 points given when trick is done on second try.
3. 100 points is a perfect contest score.
4. In the event of a tie, the winner will

be the one who can *Loop-the-Loop* the greatest number of times.

Variations on Original Rules

1. Each contestant takes a turn doing one of the "Duncan" 10 tournament tricks.
2. If the contestant does not complete a trick in 2 tries, he/she is eliminated from the contest.
3. No score is kept.
4. If more than one contestant completes the 10 tournament tricks, he/she must perform an intermediate or advanced trick in 2 tries.
5. If there still is no winner, two-handed tricks may be performed.
6. In the event that a winner cannot be determined, the champ of the neighborhood will be the one who can do one-handed or, if necessary, two-handed *Loop-the-Loops* the greatest number of times.
7. Contestant may be grouped according to age: kids, 8-14; teens, 15-20; and "kids," 21-100!

Glossary

Axle—wooden or metal shaft joining the two yo-yo halves

Back groove—yo-yo groove nearer your body

Clockwise—in the same direction as clock hands move around a clock

Counterclockwise—in the opposite direction from clockwise

Dead yo-yo—an unwound yo-yo that is not spinning

Fourth finger—the finger between the middle finger and the pinky

Free hand—hand without the yo-yo

Front groove—the groove farthest away from your body

Halves—the two sides of the yo-yo

Horizontal string—a yo-yo string that goes across from left to right or right to left.

Inside yo-yo string—the part of the string nearer your body

Loop—the figure of a yo-yo string that curves back to cross itself

Middle finger—the longest finger

Outside yo-yo string—the part of the

yo-yo string farthest away from your body

Pinky—smallest, or fifth, finger

Replacement string—yo-yo string that can be purchased to replace string on yo-yo that is worn out, knotted, or broken

Second finger—the finger between the thumb and middle finger

Sleep, or spin—the rotation of the yo-yo in circular motion at the bottom of the string

Slipknot—the loop that is placed around the middle finger at the top of the yo-yo string

Slip loop, or slip-string—the loop at the bottom of the yo-yo string that slips around the axle

String-formation, or picture-string, trick—a trick in which the yo-yo string is used to form a picture

String trick—a trick that involves using part of the yo-yo string

Yo-yo hand—hand with yo-yo

Bibliography

The following references will be of interest to those who want to know more about yo-yos.

Burger, Wolfgang. *The Yo-Yo: A Toy Flywheel. American Scientist,* March/April, 1984.

Cassidy John. *The Klutz Yo-Yo Book.* Klutz Press, 1987, Palo Alto. Available from Klutz Press Inc., 2170 Staunton Ct., Palo Alto, CA 94306.

Cohen, Martin. "The Swinging World of Yo-Yos," *Boys' Life* (December 1971).

Conroy, Frank. "A Yo-Yo Going Down, A Mad Squirrel Coming Up," *Stop Time.* New York: Penguin Books, 1967.

Dickson, Paul. *Yo-Yoing: "The Fad That Keeps Coming Back," The Mature Person's Guide to Kites, Yo-Yos, Frisbees, and Other Childlike Diversons.* New York: Plume Books, 1977.

Duncan Yo-Yo. *How to Be an Expert* video tape. PO Box 165, Baraboo, WI 53913.

Giant Book of Duncan Yo-Yo Return Top Tricks. Evanston, Illinois, 1961.

Gould, D.W. *The Top: Universal Toy, Enduring Pastime.* New York: Clarkson N. Potter, 1973.

Hoffman, Abbie. "Yo-Yo Power." *Esquire,* October, 1970.

Ives, Thomas. "How to Master Championship Tricks," *The Art of Yo-Yo Playing.* Chicago, 1950.

Malko, George. *Will There Ever Be Another Yo-Yo Champ?* Lithopinion (Summer 1970).

Malko, George. *The One and Only Yo-Yo Book.* New York: Avon Books, 1978.

McBride, Dennis. *Know-Yo, Yo-Yo Video,* 27746 N. Santa Clarita Rd., Saugus, CA 91350.

McWhirter, Norris, and Ross. *Yo-Yo, Guinness Book of World Records.* New York: Bantam Books, 1977, 1981.

NASA. *Toys in Space* video, NASA Lyndon B. Johnson Space Center, Public Information Branch/Mail Code AP3, Film/Video Distribution Library, Houston TX 77058.

Playmaxx, *Vid-e-Yo* video, 1665 E. 18th. St., suite 207, Tucson, AZ 85719.

Rule, Bob. *Yo-Yo Secrets.* Atlanta: Yo-Yo Promotions, 1971.

Smothers Brothers, *Just Say YO!,* video, Eastman Kodak, 343 State St., Bldg. 20, Rochester NY 14650.

White, P. *33 Yo-Yo Tricks* (1976). Film available through the Cleveland, Boston, and New York public libraries. Film distributed by Serious Business, 1145 Mandana Boulevard, Oakland, California 94610.

Yomega, *The Yomega Instructional Video,* 1641 N. Main St., Fall River MA 02720.

Yo-Yos, Games of the World. ed. Frederic V. Grunfield. New York: Ballatine Books, 1977.

Yo-Yo Times, The bi-monthly newsletter for the yoyo enthusiast. Available from Creative Communications Inc., PO Box 3190, Oakton, VA 22124.

Zuckerman, Edward. *Quest for the Perfect Yo-Yo.* Science Digest, July 1985.

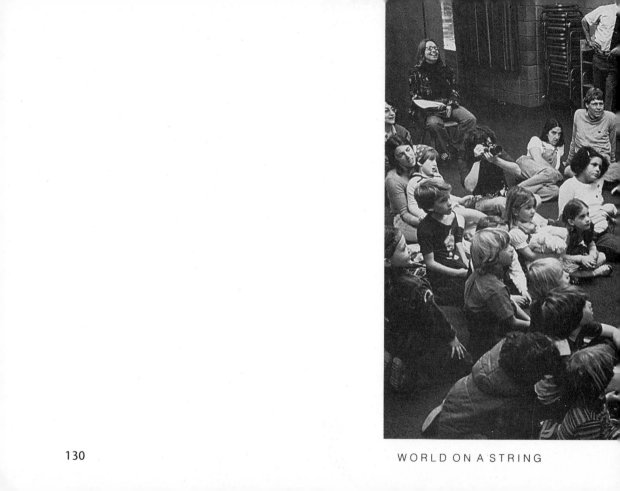

WORLD ON A STRING

Afterword

No one wants to miss a "Yo-Yo Pro" perform Chinese Puzzle.

Few books are truly finished when it is time to send them off to the publisher. There are yo-yo tricks I have purposely not included in this book. Tricks such as *Crazy Cradle, Rock-the-Baby on the Eiffel Tower, Atomic Bomb,* and *Chinese Puzzle* are still secrets of the "Yo-Yo Professionals." When they perform these tricks, their hands are faster than the eye of the average spectator. To tell you how to do them would dispel the magic and would be extremely difficult because the tricks are very complicated.

When you get to the point where you can do every trick described in this book, then it will be time for you to learn more tricks directly from the "Yo-Yo Professionals." The advanced tricks not found in this book belong to them!

Crazy Cradle.

Rock-the-Baby on the Eiffel Tower.

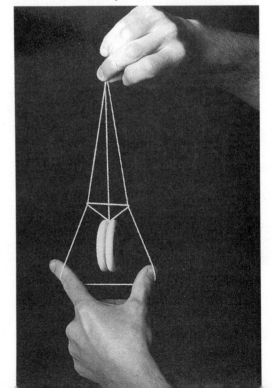

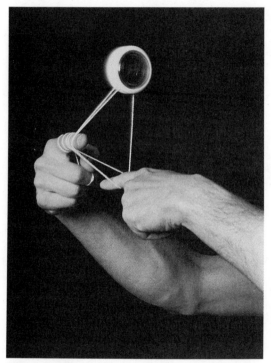

Atomic Bomb.

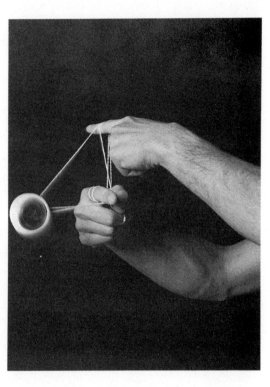

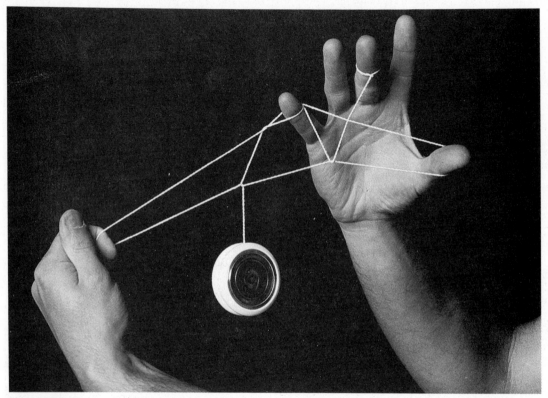

Chinese Puzzle.

Man on the Flying Trapeze Over the Wrist.

AFTERWORD

Addendum

An Update by Dr. Tom Kuhn

The past ten years have seen many developments in the world of "YO". These include improved yo-yos, yo-yos in space, a Giant yo-yo, the Smothers Brothers, and a phenomenal resurgence of interest in the sport by both children and adults.

YOYO MAKERS and SHAKERS an update:

ABZ Toys

"A good inexpensive wooden yo-yo" is what Tony Costanzo calls the Yo-Yo Pal. He worked with engineer and yoyo expert Bill DeBoisblanc to create this wooden model with a three piece construction. His yoyo sports holographic diffraction discs on the sides and a leather carrying strap which loops around the yo-yo and then slips onto the user's belt. A new high performance model is in the works. ABZ Toys Inc., 5133 Coronado Ave. Oakland, CA 94618, 415/658-9230.

American Spinners

Developer, builder and former yoyo contest winner from the Queens, New York, Bill Cress has embarked upon the business of making yoyos. He plans to market one piece wooden yoyos with exotic finishes such as metal flakes, candy apple, holographs, and dazzler designs. American Spinners, 57 Willowbrook Blvd., Suite 406, Wayne NJ 07470, 201/785-8100

Canada Games Co. Ltd.

Canada Games holds the trademark on the word "yo-yo" in Canada. The word is not generic as it is in the USA. Since purchasing the trademark from Parker Brothers two years ago, Canada games has introduced a painted wooden Pro Yo-Yo (not to be confused with Playmaxx's Pro Yo), and an Olympic Yo-Yo. Both models are of one piece wooden construction and manufactured in Sweden especially for Canada Games. Their plastic Glow Yo-Yo glows in the dark, and the Light Up model is battery operated. An Official Yo-Yo Trick Book is also available. Canada Games Company Ltd., 61 Wildcat Rd., Downsview, Ontario, Canada M3J 2P5 416/661-6203

Duncan Toys Inc.

For most people in the USA, Duncan is still synonomous for *Yo-Yo*. The line of plastic yo-yos still includes the ever popular Imperial, as well as the Wheels and Butterfly Yo-Yos. The new Mel Yo Dee musical yo-yo plays the Duncan jingle when spun while the Satellite may still be the best electric yoyo made. As the yo-yo is thrown, the centrifugal force trips a switch which lights it up. Nothing can compare to the Satellite's visual effect for yo-yoing in the dark. Another new model is called the Gold Award Yo-Yo. which is filled with dazzling gold metal flakes. In Duncan's instructional video called "How to Be an Expert," yo-yo and spin top champion Tom Parks guides the viewer from the basics through the complex moves. Duncan Toys Inc., P.O. Box 165, Baraboo, WI 53913, 608/356-5551

Hummingbird Toy Company

Brad Countryman started out as a wood carver and furniture maker. Making carousel animals, and fancy furniture left him with lots of wood scraps. The wood being too nice to waste, he turned some of those scraps into beautiful rare wood yo-yos which he began to market through various museum gift shops. The response was so encouraging that in 1983, Brad introduced a less expensive yo-yo called the Hummingbird Classic. It's made of domestic hard maple, a wood which is optimally weighted for a professional class

The Hummingbird Toy Company makes an array of finely crafted wooden yo-yos, many with colorful laminated layers and spectacular painted finishes. (Photo courtesy Brad Countryman.)

yo-yo. Since then his furniture making has had to take a back seat to the business of making yo-yos - lots of them! His finely crafted wooden yo-yos have a three piece glued construction. Several models are beautifully painted, and others have stunning laminated wood designs. These include The Limited, Classic, Trickster, Starburst, and Wizard . He is the maker of the "Official Yo-Yo Man Yo-Yo" for the Smothers Brothers which is a custom version of the painted Starburst Yo-Yo. Hummingbird Toy Company Ltd.,32 Water St., Arcade, NY 14009, 716/492-5120.

The Klutz Company

John Cassidy is a guy who has capitalized on his own ineptitude by creating a series of instructional books designed to appeal to the Klutz in all of us. It started with the highly successful Juggling for the Complete Klutz and most recently, The Klutz Yo-Yo Book. Yo-Yo books are hard to find and here is 83 pages packed with yo-yo history, tricks, illustrations and fun — well worth owning. A Klutz maple yo-yo is packaged with each book. Klutz Press Inc., 2170 Staunton Ct., Palo Alto, CA 94306, 415/857-0888.

Klutz has taken on the yo-yo in this fun filled 83 page compendium of yo-yo tricks and history. A Klutz maple yo-yo is included with each book.

WORLD ON A STRING

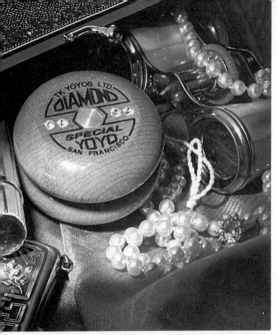

The Diamond Special Yo-Yo. (Photo by Alan Krosnick.)

The Flying Camel Yo-Yo. (Photo by Alan Krosnick.)

Tom Kuhn Custom Yo-Yos

It has been said that the resurgence of wooden yo-yos and adult involvement in the sport has been sparked by San Francisco dentist and yo-yo entrepreneur Tom Kuhn (hey - that's me!). Since its inception in 1978, the company has dedicated itself to making state-of-the-art yo-yos. Each yo-yo is carefully turned, hand sanded, finished, and performance tested. John Cassidy, author of The Klutz Yo-Yo Book (see above) has described the yoyos as looking like "small pieces of flying furniture," with an "heirloom quality." The patented modular design is incorporated into most models and allows the yoyos to be taken apart for easy access to tangles as well as replacement of the wooden axle sleeves, when needed. The No Jive 3-in-1, the first and still most popular model may be assembled in 3 different configurations — with the halves reversed, stacked piggyback, or in the classic style. The Flying Camel Yo-Yo, Mandala Yo-Yos, and autographed Smo-Bro-Yo-Yo are ornate lasercarved versions of the No Jive, while the Diamond Special is an elegant rhinestone studded yo-yo made to commemorate a yoyo that I won in my teen years. The Beginners Yo-Yo and new Woody have a 3—piece glued construction. The only non-wooden model

The Silver Bullet Yo-Yo. (Photo by Alan Krosnick.)

Patented modular design of the No Jive 3-in-1 Yo-Yo. (Photo by Dwight Van Meter.)

is the Silver Bullet Yo-Yo which is made of aircraft quality aluminum with replaceable wooden axles. This long spinner has been called the Ferarri of Yo-Yos. Also available are tee shirts and two videos: The 30 minute Smother's Brothers instructional video called "Just Say YO!," and the 53 minute video tape by "Yo-ologist" Dennis McBride called the "Know-Yo, Yo-Yo Video." Tom Kuhn Custom Yo-Yos Ltd., 2383 California St., San Francisco CA 94115, 415/921-8138.

Playmaxx

Yo-yo pioneer Don Duncan Jr. is still making those long spinning Pro-Yos, described earlier in the book, but the company name is now Playmaxx instead of Duracraft. In an interview published in the Yo-Yo Times (April-May 1988), Duncan perceives yo-yos as sporting goods as much as toys. He states, "It's challenging, it takes skill to operate and learn, its competitive, it teaches hand-eye coordination and it gives the user a sense of accomplishment". He also mentions that "the key to a good working yo-yo is the relationship between the width of the string groove, the string and the size of the axle. If the relationship is correct, the yo-yo works beautifully. If not, it's frustrating for the kid." Don Duncan's newest product is called the Ad-Yo, which is basically a Pro-Yo which may be customized by imprinting messages or company logos on the sides of the halves. Also available is the Playmaxx "Vid-e-Yo," an instructional tape featuring long time yo-yo professional, Dale Oliver Playmaxx Inc., 1665 E. 18th St., Suite 207, Tucson, AZ 85719, 602/623-9981

The Jack Russell Company

Jack Russell was a Duncan Yo-Yo professional back in the heyday of the sport. He started a company that most people in the USA have never heard of, and yet The Jack Russell Company just might be the largest volume yoyo company in the world. For decades they have run worldwide promotions for the Coca Cola Company and manufacture many popular and high performing plastic yoyos with the Coca Cola logos. His promotions are well coordinated efforts with large teams of demonstrators fanning out over countries near and far, although promotions in the USA have been discontinued for lack of interest. Daniel Volk, a former Russell demonstrator has described the joys of introducing yo-yos to areas even as remote as New Guinea, where no one had ever seen them before. The Jack Russell Company has helped make yo-yoing an extremely popular sport throughout the world. The Jack Russell Co., 465 Riverside Dr., Stuart, FL 34996, 407/287-1377.

The Smothers Brothers

The Smothers Brothers have been a comedy team since the 1960's and the popular Smothers Brothers Comedy Hour television show and night club act has a featured segment where Tommy is "The YoYo Man" while brother Dick challenges him to perform the tricks flawlessly. This popular segment of their show has created a new generation of yoyo fans and yoyo fever all over the nation. I met Tom Smothers in 1984 and since then we have spent many enjoyable hours together in the "State of YO." We got acquainted when his brother Dick bought him a No Jive Yo-Yo which he liked and began to use in his act. Tom and Dick have sanctioned two versions of their own Smothers Brothers Yo-Yo. A beautifully painted glued wooden version with a gold stamped trademark is made by the Hummingbird Toy Company of Arcade, New York. The classy laser-carved autograph Smo-Bro-Yo-Yo with high performance modular design (like the No Jive YoYo) is offered by Tom Kuhn Custom Yoyos of San Francisco. Recently The Smothers Brothers have completed an instructional video called "Just Say YO!" which is a delightful 30 minute romp through the fundamental and more advanced states of yo-yoing starring Tommy Smothers (The Yo-Yo

The Official Yo-Yo Man Yo-Yo is made by the Hummingbird Toy Co. (Photo courtesy Brad Countryman.)

Man), Daniel Volk (The YO Master), and Dick Smothers (The Voice of Yo). Available from Eastman Kodak Videos, 343 State St., Bldg 20, Rochester NY 14650 or Tom Kuhn Custom Yo-Yos (415) 921-8138.

Spinmaster International

Carl Bates has started a company marketing a plastic yo-yo which he states is designed to look and perform like the old wooden Duncan Tournaments. Bates has been involved in yo-yoing for 35 years and wants to encourage kids by staging contests in his area. Spinmaster International, 6800 Westgate Blvd., Suite 139B-207, Austin, TX 78745, 512/444-6669.

Yomega Corporation

Yomega — The Yo-Yo with a Brain was invented by Michael Caffrey. It has a spring activated clutch which automatically returns the yo-yo to the hand when the yo-yo slows to a critical speed. It was developed to alleviate the frustration younger children

Tom and Dick Smothers getting into the Yo-Yo groove. (Photo courtesy Smothers Brothers Comedy Hour.)

om Kuhn ("Dr. YO") and Tom Smothers ("The Yo-Yo Man") in the State of "YO"
*hoto courtesy Smothers Brothers Comedy Hour.)

ADDENDUM

experience while learning yo-yo tricks. Company president Alan Amaral describes the Yomega as being long spinning and modular allowing the yoyo to come apart for access to knots. The Yomega is available in two versions, the Phantom and the Executive model which sports polished brass accents. Yomega owners Len and Alan Amaral are featured in "The Yomega Instructional Video." Yomega Corp., 1641 N. Main St., Fall River, MA 02720. 617/672-7399.

The Yo-Yo Times

Stuart Crump is an expert on cellular phones and electronic communications systems, but he has also described himself as a "confirmed yo-yo nut!" Yearning for more information about the sport and lore of yo-yos, he decided that a newsletter would be the best way to obtain and share the latest information. So he launched The Yo-Yo Times in the Spring of 1988, with the headline article appropriately entitled "How to Prosper in a Yo-Yo Economy." The publication features many new yo-yo tricks and tips, as well as what's new in products. There are letters to the editor and spotlights on yo-yo personalities. A must for every serious Yo-er. Yo-Yo Times, PO Box 3190, Oakton, VA 22124, 703/648-9060 or 703/758-9696

The Yomega is the only yo-yo with a built in clutch which returns the yo-yo automatically as the rpm's slow to a critical point. (Photo courtesy Alan Amaral.)

WORLD ON A STRING

THE NO JIVE YOYO STORY
A quest for the perfect yo-yo.

In 1976 I received a wooden yoyo as a gift. I hadn't seen one since my school days in Detroit, Michigan in the fifties. The yoyo broke on the first day and my attempts at fixing it started my "Quest For The Perfect Yo-yo" (see *Science Digest* July 1985). Using a jig saw and electric drill with sandpaper, I finished the first yo-yo in time for a European vacation. It looked crude, but was such a good traveling companion that on returning, my goal was to make the best yo-yo possible for myself.

I got down to the fundamentals of yo-yo esthetics and physics — what is a yo-yo's optimum weight, shape, string groove, and axle? The axles on wooden yo-yos were typically 1/4 inch or thicker, but I discovered that narrower axles meant longer spins. However, if they were too narrow, the yo-yo wouldn't loop as well and the axle would be too weak. A yo-yo which is a good looper as well as a long spinner requires some careful compromises of design. Trial and error led to a 50 gram maple prototype yo-yo that I called "1," the predecessor of the No Jive Yo-Yo. It was hard to put this yo-yo down! I made about 25 duplicates for gifts that year and branded them with a Maple Leaf "No Jive Yo-Yo" die.

The trade-off for 1's narrower high performance axle was strength, and within a few weeks string friction weakened old 1 to the verge of breaking. I quit playing with it and realized that the next model would have to be more durable. I still wanted the feel of wood but would compromise on an unbreakable axle, so I tried steel, brass, and aluminum. I was baffled that none of the variously designed metal axles worked as well as old 1.

Six key stages in the development of the No Jive 3-in-1 with the 1st yo-yo ever made by Tom Kuhn followed by Old 1, No Jive Maple Leaf, Prototype with brass axle, and prototype with hex nut and wooden axle, and the final product (left). Array of some of the prototype axle designs for the No Jive (below left). Thirty of the numerous prototypes used in developing the No Jive 3-in-1 Yo-Yo. The three assembly configurations are seen in the bottom row (below). (Photos by Alan Krosnick.)

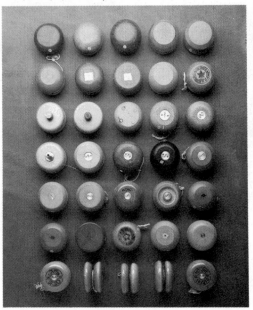

The No Jive 3-in-1 Yo-Yo. (Photo by Alan Krosnick.)

ADDENDUM

A dental patient of mine suggested that NASA had materials data from the space program available to the public. Perhaps they could shed light on the ideal yo-yo axle material. I opened my briefcase full of yo-yo prototypes and described the problem to Dr. Walter Goldenrath a research director at NASA Ames Research Center in Mountain View, California: Was there a material that would react like wood does with a cotton yoyo string and yet be stronger? Within weeks I received samples of space age Teflons and other materials from various NASA suppliers that I turned into yoyo axles. None surpassed the performance of good old 1!

The solution became clear: Build a yoyo with a *replaceable wooden axle* reinforced with a steel screw for strength. Shape it like 1 and make it easy to dismantle for access to tangles and knots. Design it to reassemble in three different ways and you have the No Jive 3-in-1 Yo-Yo! I liked it, felt the world desperately needed it, and started a yo-yo company. Over the years, people have sent many encouraging fan letters, and yes, 12 years later I'm still playing with them myself.

YO-YOS and THE SPACE PROGRAM

In September 1984 the NASA/Yo-Yo connection continued and I got a chance to pay NASA back for helping to develop the No Jive Yo-yo axle. I sent three yo-yos and a recommendation for a "Yo-yos in Space" experiment to NASA in Houston. On February 4, 1985 I heard a radio report that a yo-yo was to go into space. Why hadn't they called? I located the organizer of the upcoming "Toys in Space Experiment," who had purchased the toys for the project. She hadn't heard of my letter, but told me that Astronaut David Griggs was responsible for yo-yoing on the flight. I express shipped a new batch of yo-yos to him.

Astronaut David Griggs getting some pointers from Tom Kuhn. (Photo by Kim Connor.)

In the pilots compartment of the space shuttle simulator. (Photo by Kim Connor.)

Two days later during dinner, the phone rang and I was amazed to be talking to the Astronaut himself! Just out of a full day in a shuttle trainer, he called to let me know how impressed and delighted he was with the yo-yos that he had received. We talked about his upcoming mission, and I volunteered to help with yo-yos and advice. The lesson sounded like a good idea, and Astronaut Griggs called back the following day to invite me to the Johnson Space Center. I flew there the following week (at my own expense - for you worried taxpayers).

I felt awkward tripping over U.S. Senator Jake Garn who was training in the somewhat cramped shuttle simulator, as

I dragged my cameras, home video gear, and yoyos up to the pilots compartment. Astronaut Griggs demonstrated the space shuttle's many incredible features. Then the day's work started in earnest. Using No Jive and Silver Bullet Yo-Yos, we practiced maneuvers that he would attempt on the flight. Other astronauts on the simulator and in the offices were also caught up in the "YO energy." By day's end Astronaut Griggs was confident that he could handle this part of his next space mission.

Shuttle flight STS 51-D majestically took off with its payload April 12, 1985 and returned on April 19. I spoke with David Griggs barely 24 hours later. This wonderful rocket man's descriptions of the bone jolting take off, whisper silent re-entry, transcendental space walk, and views of Earth and heavens were enthusiastic and poetic. He also said that the yoyo was a popular device with the astronauts in their isolation, and that it demonstrated unusual behavior in space.

For purposes of fire safety, a yellow plastic Duncan Imperial Yo-Yo was equipped with a stiffer fireproof kevlar string. It would not "sleep" no matter how loose the string was nor how hard or soft he threw it. When the yoyo bottomed out, a slight stretching of the string occurred and without gravity to keep the yoyo down it would return to his hand every time. This has been termed the "G bonk" by NASA scientist and yo-yo aficionado Don Pettit of the Los Alamos test laboratory in New Mexico (more about him later).

Dynamic tricks did work, and David Griggs' most fascinating discoveries were the slow motion tricks, where the yoyo would spin even as slow as 3 or 4 rpms, allowing close scrutiny of the yo-yo and string. If the yo-yo was heading off course,

Astronaut David Griggs yo-yos in space on flight 51-D. (Photo courtesy of NASA.)

mid-flight corrections could easily be made by appropriately tugging the string. This helped with dynamic tricks like "Reach for the Moon" - a trick he couldn't do on earth, but could do on the shuttle. Video tapes of the flight show a gleeful expression as Griggs performed this and other difficult maneuvers with ease. Copies of the "Toys in Space Video" (#CMP 211) may be borrowed by writing: NASA Lyndon B. Johnson Space Center, Public Information Branch/Mail Code AP3, Film/Video Distribution Library, Houston TX 77058, 713/486-9606

Quest for the Ideal Zero Gravity (0g) Yo-Yo

Don Pettit is a research engineer at the Los Alamos National Laboratory in New Mexico. He flies routinely with NASA on the KC-135 planes, which fly parabolic trajectories that create short periods of weightlessness. His studies involve zero-gravity fluid dynamics. He also likes yo-yos and in bits of free time on his weightless flights, he has done his own research on zero-gravity (Og) yoyo dynamics. He has discovered that to compensate for the zero "g bonk," a short sleeper can be thrown which he calls "The Snoozer." He writes: "Throw yo-yo as usual for Og, and before it reaches end of the string, accelerate hand (slowly) backward in a straight line away from the yo-yo. This will give a small g force, allowing yoyo to "snooze" for a couple of seconds, until arm reaches limit of travel and rolls back." The other way to make a yoyo sleep in space was to do "Around the World," where the orbiting yoyo creates its own artificial gravity. Don Pettit firmly believes that a yo-yo could do wonders for crew morale on long manned space flights, so the unofficial research continues to create the ideal Og yoyo.

THE WORLD'S BIGGEST YOYO

Bob Haas is a fourth-generation owner of a San Francisco company called Haas Wood and Ivory Works that specializes in wooden ornamentations for Victorian houses. He and his crew were captivated by the idea of building a giant scaled-up version of the No Jive 3-in-1 Yo-Yo. The project required laminating 220 board feet of California sugar pine as well as Baltic birch (from the U.S.S.R.) for the faces. The yo-yo halves were meticulously turned to scale on a giant lathe and then connected by an axle assembly just like the pocket sized version. The finished Big-YO is a 256 pound replica measuring 50 inches tall and 31 1/2 inches wide. The "string" that was selected is 3/4 inch braided Dacron rope with a rated tensile strength of 11,600 pounds. The first secret test launch occurred in late 1979, when the yo-yo was released from a 100 foot crane at a yacht harbor in San Rafael

Winding the 3/4 inch diameter dacron "string" around the World's Biggest Yo-Yo. (Photo by Ed Kashi.)

California.

To date, the yo-yo has been launched on four occasions over sea and land.

The only failure was a spectacular one that occurred in 1980 during a launch off Pier 39 in San Francisco. The rope was mistakenly lubricated with water prior to this launch. A huge crowd — local news cameras and a "You Asked For It" camera crew — were all trained on the yoyo as it was hoisted 120 feet over the water. There

157

was a hush from the crowd, the safety sling was released, and the yoyo came down, building up terrific rotational speed. When it reached the end of the rope. it was spinning furiously. I signaled to the crane operator to jerk the yoyo up, but the yoyo wouldn't respond to the crane's repeated tugs as it did on the test

"It's a U.F.YO!" (Photo by Ed Kashi.)

launching. Just like a yoyo whose string is too loose or over waxed, it kept spinning. Steam started spewing from the axle groove! When the 454 degree Fahrenheit melting point of the rope was reached, it melted through and Big-YO fell 30 feet down and splashed into San Francisco Bay where it started floating out to sea.

Frogman Ken Cochrane heroically jumped in and swam to the bobbing yoyo before it drifted too far. He lassoed and towed it back to the pier where the crane hoisted it out of the water. By now the camera teams had packed up and left, but I was sure we could make it work on the second try.

SPLASH!
(Photo by Owen Brewer.)

Diver Ken Cockrane rescues BIG-YO and tows it back to shore. (Photo by Owen Brewer.)

It was heartwarming to see most of the crowd stay and pitch in to dismantle, shake out, and meticulously dry the slippery yoyo halves with gobs of paper towels donated from a nearby restaurant.

This time a fresh dry rope was <u>tied</u> to the axle, the yoyo wound and hoisted to the top of the crane. Again it was released, rolling downward, building up speed. When it reached the bottom, it majestically shot 3/4 of the way back up the rope to the cheers of the crowd and continued to "Yo" for 6 or 7 times. A color photo of this yoyo may be seen in the 1981 hardcover edition of the Guinness Book of World Records.

On the second try it YO-ed majestically up and down.
(Photo by Owen Brewer.)

The State of "Yo"

The State of "Yo" is a blissful state of being where the distinctions between the player, the yo-yo and the trick disappear. It happens when we become fascinated by, and attentive to, the spinning yo-yo, and immersed in the trick. Our hands and bodies choreograph a dance — the yo-yo is our partner. The tricks need not be complex. I have seen beginners so focused on the basic up and down movement that the effect is elegant and graceful.

To enter the State of "Yo" is to understand why yo-yos have captivated millions throughout the ages. Ask the kids in the school yard why they like to yo-yo and they'll say "Its fun." The busy executive with a phone in one hand and a yo-yo in the other might reply "Its soothing". In The State of "Yo" we are uncluttered by problems and grounded in the present moment. This is the secret of its charm.

Tom Kuhn in the State of YO. (Photo by Cheryl Lynne Pickens.)

"Could you show me that again? I always get the string caught in my antlers!" (Photo by Leon Ilnicki.)

WORLD ON A STRING

Index

NOTES

NOTES

TOM KUHN CUSTOM YO-YOS BY MAIL

MANDALA YO-YO
-intricate lasercarving-
Meditation in Motion

SILVER BULLET YO-YO
-includes leather holster-
The Longest Spinner

DIAMOND SPECIAL
YO-YO
Watch it sparkle!

FLYING CAMEL YO-YO
-Model F-
Flies thru the Tricks!

SMO-BRO YO-YO
Official Smothers Brothers
Autograph Yo-Yo

NO JIVE 3-in-1 YO-YO
Assembles 3 Ways

Illustrations by Ellery Knight.

TOM KUHN CUSTOM YO-YOS
2383 California Street
San Francisco, CA 94115

ORDER FORM

QUANTITY	DESCRIPTION	PRICE	TOTAL
	No Jive 3-in-1 Yo-Yo	$18.00	
	Mandala Yo-Yo	20.00	
	Flying Camel Yo-Yo - Model F *(carved on flat side)*	20.00	
	Flying Camel Yo-Yo - Model C *(carved on curved side)*	20.00	
	Diamond Special Yo-Yo	25.00	
	Silver Bullet Yo-Yo	40.00	
	Smothers Brothers Autographed Yo-Yo	22.50	
	Smothers Brothers Yo-Yo Man Video *(38 min.)*	12.00	
	Dennis McBride's "Know-Yo" Video *(53 min.)*	25.00	
	ALL OF ABOVE* + *bonus* Beginner's Yo-Yo (8 yo-yos & 2 tapes)	$175.00	
	Shipping all orders		$2.50
	Overseas Shipping Add $5.00		
	Calif. Residents Add 6% TAX		
	TOTAL		

HAPPY YO-ing!

SHIP TO:

Name _____

Address _____

City/State _____ Zip _____

Telephone ( ) _____

Pay by check, money order or

VISA/MC # _____ Exp. Date _____

Please allow 3-4 weeks for delivery.

PHONE ORDERS: 415/921-8138

All Yo-Yos include:
• 60-ft. string spool
• extra axles
• instruction booklet

NO JIVE 3-in-1 YO-YO

NOTES